THE ROMANCE OF
THE RED TRIANGLE

Y.M.C.A. AND GERMAN OBSERVATION STATION IN THE TREES
AT ACHIET-LE-PETIT

THE ROMANCE

OF THE

RED TRIANGLE

THE STORY OF THE COMING OF THE
RED TRIANGLE AND THE SERVICE
RENDERED BY THE Y.M.C.A. TO THE
SAILORS AND SOLDIERS OF THE
BRITISH EMPIRE

BY

SIR ARTHUR K. YAPP, K.B.E.

Illustrations by
W. P. STARMER, EDGAR WRIGHT
AND OTHER ARTISTS

HODDER AND STOUGHTON
LONDON   NEW YORK   TORONTO

DEDICATION

*THIS book is affectionately dedicated to Y.M.C.A.
leaders and workers at home and abroad in grateful appreciation of their faithful and loyal service.
Much of this work has been done out of sight, and
endless difficulties have had to be surmounted.
Names have not been mentioned in the book, but
the writer would like to express his personal
gratitude and appreciation to every one.*

411943

CONTENTS

CONTENTS

CONTENTS

CHAPTER XVI

CHAPTER XVII

CHAPTER XVIII

LIST OF · ILLUSTRATIONS ·

LIST OF ILLUSTRATIONS xiii

CHAPTER I

THE COMING OF THE RED TRIANGLE

His Majesty congratulates the Association on the successful results of its war work, which has done everything conducive to the comfort and well-being of the armies, supplying the special and peculiar needs of men drawn from countries so different and distant. It has worked in a practical, economical and unostentatious manner, with consummate knowledge of those with whom it has to deal. At the same time the Association, by its spirit of discipline, has earned the respect and approbation of the military authorities.—HIS MAJESTY THE KING.

IT was in the summer of 1901, in the old volunteer days, that the Y.M.C.A. for the first time had its recreation tents at Conway in North Wales. The Lancashire Fusiliers were in camp, and the men had thronged the marquee all day, turning up in great force for the service that Sunday evening. It seemed as if they would never tire of singing the old familiar hymns, and when the time

A

came for the address the attention of every man was riveted from start to finish. At length the tent cleared, and the men retired for the night. Now and then the chorus of a hymn could be heard coming from a bell tent, but soon the 'Last Post' sounded, and a few minutes later the plaintive notes of the bugle gave the signal for 'Lights Out.' Thereupon two of the Y.M.C.A. leaders, leaving the camp behind, walked up and down the sands of Morfa. It was a perfect night ; not a sound was to be heard except the gentle ripple of the waves, three or four hundred yards away. The moon was near the full ; everything seemed almost as light as day, and the bold outline of the Conway Mountain stood in clear relief against the sky. ' I wonder what all this means,' said one of the two, referring to the impressive service of the evening and to the crowds that had thronged the tents all day. ' I have been wondering,' said he, ' if there is a great European war looming in the distance, and if God is preparing the Y.M.C.A. for some great work it is destined to perform then.' How often have those words come back since the beginning of the war ! God was indeed preparing the Association for a work infinitely bigger than any of its leaders knew or even dared to hope. In those days H.R.H. the Duke of Connaught became Patron of our Military Camp Department, and he has ever since been a warm friend..

How far distant now seem those early days of August 1914. For weeks there had been rumours of war, but all arrangements had been completed for the work of the Y.M.C.A. in the Territorial camps to proceed as usual during the August holidays. Then came the order for mobilisation, and on August the 4th a council of war was held at Headquarters, attended by Association leaders from all parts of the country.

Many of the districts were in financial difficulties, owing to the sudden break up of
the summer camps, and the only possible
policy was the one agreed upon at the
meeting—a common programme and a
common purse. No one knew where the
men, or the money, were to come from, but
it was decided to go right ahead, and from
that resolve there could be no turning back.
It is still true that ' He that saveth his life
shall lose it, and he that loseth his life shall
find it.' In that great crisis, had the
leaders of the Y.M.C.A. stopped to consider
first the immediate or future interests of
the Association, then the Association would
have gone under, and deservedly so.
Britain was in danger, and her interests
had to be considered first.

What stirring days those were! We
think of one tiny village to the south-west
of Salisbury Plain, with a normal popula-
tion of two or three hundred. Within a

few days of the opening of hostilities, thirty-four thousand men were dumped down in the immediate vicinity. They had no tents, no uniforms, no rifles, nowhere to go, and nothing to do, for the simple reason that England did not desire war and had not prepared for it. The General in command had known the Y.M.C.A. in India, and came to London to ask our help, which was gladly given. Huge recreation tents were opened there, and all over the country. North, South, East, and West, Britain was suddenly transformed into one armed camp, and the Y.M.C.A. was never more needed than it was in those early days. Some of the centres were very small, others very large. At the Y.M.C.A. in the White City, for instance, it was no uncommon thing to see four or five thousand men gathered together in the great hall. At the Crystal Palace, too, and in many of the camps, the work was carried out on a very large

scale, whilst in other centres a farm building,
a private house, or a tiny tent met the need.

Thanks to the loyal co-operation and
energy of Association leaders and workers,
two hundred and fifty of these centres were
established within ten days. They were
dotted down all over the country, and every
week that passed by showed an increase in
strength and in the number of centres,
until the sign of the Red Triangle was to be
found in more than two thousand centres in
all parts of the United Kingdom, in every
part of the Empire, on every battle-front,
and in some places where the Allied flags
do not yet fly. The hands of the Military
in those days were so full up with other
things that they had little time to devote
to the recreation of the troops, and our help
was warmly welcomed. We have acted
throughout in close co-operation with the
Military, and we should like to add our
tribute of praise to the efficiency of the

Military machine, as we have come in touch with it. Much has been said during the war as to the marvels of German organisation, and possibly not too much. At the same time there is quite as much to be said in praise of British organisation. Germany wanted a war whilst we did not. Germany prepared for war, tirelessly, ceaselessly; with her eye on the goal—world-wide dominion—she brought all her organising ability to bear on the preparation for the war she was determined to force on humanity. Britain, on the other hand, has had to improvise her war organisation since war has been actually forced on her. A run round the great base camps in France will show how wonderfully complete is that organisation—transport, supply, commissariat. Of course there have been mistakes, but singularly few under the circumstances. Many people are very critical of the War Office, but those who know most of the

difficulties that have been overcome and
the successes achieved, will be the least inclined to join hands with the critics.

It is like a nightmare to think of that
first winter of the war, with its gales, rain
and mud, and it was when the weather was
at its worst that the men of the first
Canadian Contingent were encamped on
Salisbury Plain.   It is difficult to conceive
what they would have done, but for the
timely help of the Red Triangle.   The roads
were almost impassable, and the mud in
the vicinity of the camps appalling, but
the Canadians stuck it, and so did our
leaders and workers.   The tents were
crowded to their utmost capacity, but it
was soon found that no tent could weather
the gales of Salisbury Plain in winter.
That discovery led to the evolution of the
Y.M.C.A. hut.   Wooden frames covered
with canvas were tried first of all, but they,
too, were incapable of withstanding the

fury of the gales, and something much stronger had to be provided.

It meant a great deal to the country during that first winter of the war that the men were happy and contented, because they had their leisure hours pleasantly occupied, and because the most popular place in camp was almost without exception the one that bore the sign of the Red Triangle. And what did they find at the sign of the Red Triangle? They found there an open house, a warm welcome, a place of recreation and enjoyment, where they could meet their friends on terms thoroughly cordial and unofficial. Coffee and buns were always a great attraction, and as for music—the piano was hardly ever silent. Tommy Atkins loves a good tune and loves a crowd; the quiet place does not so much appeal to him. At the Y.M.C.A. he found diversion for his hours of leisure; opportunity for study if he

cared for it ; libraries, classes, and lectures.
There, too, he found an expression of
religious life that appealed to him, the
inspiration that comes from religion without
the controversy and sectarian bitterness
which, alas! too often accompany it, a
religion to work by and a religion that can
do things. Before the war nobody had
heard of our mystic sign, but within a few
weeks letters bearing it had found their
way into hundreds of thousands of homes,
bringing joy and consolation wherever they
went. That, in brief, is the story of the
coming of the Red Triangle. And what is
its significance ? As the emblem of the
war work of the Y.M.C.A. it has not been
chosen by chance, but because it exactly
typifies the movement it represents. The
threefold needs of men are its concern, and
its programme is adapted to meet the needs
of body, mind, and spirit, whilst its colour
symbolises sacrifice. In an old book of

signs and wonders called *Mysterium Magnum*
the inverted triangle appears as a symbol of
the divine spirit, and in the third year of
the war a famous Belgian painter asked
' Qu'est-ce-que c'est—cet Y.M.C.A. ? ' and
without waiting for an answer went on to
say that the Red Triangle meant emblem-
atically—' Spirit informing and penetrating
matter,' which was, he supposed, the function of the Y.M.C.A. ' The Y.M.C.A. is
attempting the impossible,' said one of its
critics ; ' it is building on the apex of the
triangle.' Thank God it is. Yes ! and
thank God it has achieved the impossible.
If any one had dared to foretell four years
ago, a tithe of what has already been
accomplished, no one would have believed
it. The secret of the inverted triangle is
that it is upheld by invisible hands, and it
is the full programme of the Red Triangle
that appeals so irresistibly to the men.
If we were merely out to run a canteen,

others could perhaps have done the canteen work as well, or nearly as well, as the Y.M.C.A. Others could run lectures for the troops, and others cater for their spiritual needs, but it has been left to the Y.M.C.A. to formulate the appeal to the whole man—Body, Mind, and Spirit— and the appeal to every man, irrespective of creed or party. Every man is equally welcome in the Y.M.C.A.—Protestant, Romanist, Anglican, Free-churchman, Jew, Mohammedan, Buddhist, Hindoo, or Brahmin—the men of every religion and no religion, and yet the religious note is ever dominant, though no man's religion will ever be attacked from a Y.M.C.A. platform.

The story of the Red Triangle is, indeed, one of the great romances of the war. Its work has never been regarded as an end in itself, but rather as auxiliary to that of other organisations. It is auxiliary to the Church, and its doors have been thrown wide open to the Padres of all denominations. Protestants, Catholics, Jews—even Mohammedans—have worshipped God in their own way within the hospitable walls of the Association. It has been auxiliary to the official medical services of the Army, the R.A.M.C., and the Red Cross—in hospitals and convalescent camps, and with the walking wounded at the clearing stations at the Front. It has arranged concerts and entertainments by the thousand for patients and nurses ; has looked after the friends of dangerously wounded men, and has often handed over its huts to be used as emergency hospitals ; while in hosts of other ways which can never be recorded, it has been able to render vitally important service. It has been auxiliary to the Military machine at every turn of the war. In the midst of the camp though not of it, its secretaries and workers conform to military rules and are subject to discipline, although they are themselves civilians. In this way the Association has provided the human touch, and officers and men alike have appreciated the fact that there is one place in camp where discipline through being temporarily relaxed, has been permanently strengthened.

The Romance of the Red Triangle, like the story of the first crusade, has been the romance of the pioneer. The Y.M.C.A. was first in the field, though now there are many other organised societies and private individuals doing similar work on the lines which it thought out and proved to be practicable. Indeed, the whole story of the Y.M.C.A. has been full of adventurous episodes of romance, not merely during the war, but long before it, commencing seventy years ago, when George Williams came as a boy from Somerset to London, and as one of a band of twelve intrepid young men, founded the first branch of a movement destined to spread to all corners of the world. It is only during these years of war that the Society has fully come into its own, and received universal recognition, but we do not forget that to those pioneers of the early Victorian days and to the Y.M.C.A. leaders, who during the years before the war hammered out a policy for work amongst soldiers in the Volunteer and Territorial camps, the widespread movement of to-day is largely due.

To know what the Army thinks of the Y.M.C.A., one need only note, on the one hand, the facilities given to the Association by officers in high command ; and on the other, how the N.C.O.'s and men—officers and officer-cadets too—make use of the huts.

Prior to one of our great advances in 1917, the district to be attacked was

reconstructed behind the line in a large
map carefully worked out on the ground,
every road and path being clearly marked.
Every trench, redoubt, and dug-out;
every hedge and ditch was recorded, and
every gun emplacement shown. ' Reserved
for the Y.M.C.A.' was written over a
vacant plot near the centre of the map.

In France ' Le Triangle Rouge ' is often
called ' Les Ygrecs ' (The Y's), and the
Red Triangle will pass the Association
worker almost anywhere. It sounds odd
in the reserve trenches, amidst the roar of
guns and the scream of shells, to hear the
sentry's challenge as we have heard it,
' Halt ! who goes there ? ' ' Y.M.C.A.'
' Pass, Y.M., all 's well ! '

One of our workers in the valley of the
Somme in 1917 was left behind, as the
troops advanced to follow up the line of
the great German retreat. For weeks he
shared his Y.M.C.A. shanty with the rats,

HUT IN THE GROUNDS OF THE RUINS OF THE HÔTEL-DE-VILLE AT ARRAS

ONE OF MANY Y.M.C.A. HUTS BUILT UNDER SHELL-FIRE

and late one evening went for a two miles walk. A sentry challenged him, and evidently regarded him with suspicion. After he had convinced the guard of his identity, it was explained to him that three German prisoners were at large, and one of them was known to be wearing a Y.M.C.A. uniform. When he awoke that night in his rat-infested shanty it seemed to him that if the three Huns chanced to know of his whereabouts, it would not be a difficult thing for them to possess themselves of yet another Y.M.C.A. uniform!

In the early days of the war it was agreed that no request for the help of the Association, which on investigation proved a definite need to exist, should be refused, and God honoured the faith of those who dared to make the resolve. The way the movement has grown and is growing still is nothing short of a romance, and the following pages tell the story of service rendered under the sign of the Red Triangle to the men of His Majesty's Forces, irrespective of class, creed, or party, in England and north of the Border, in Wales and Ireland, on every battle-front and in every base ;- amongst men of every colour and creed who are serving under our great Flag—the Flag that stands for Freedom.

Possibly the greatest romance of all will be that dealing with the work of the Red Triangle after the war.   Who knows ?

CHAPTER II

BLAZING THE TRAIL WITH THE RED TRIANGLE

Few organisations have done so much in caring for the comfort and well-being of our soldiers as your Associations. They have given invaluable help to the Army, and have immeasurably lightened the hardships which have to be endured by our troops. In recognising the excellent work that has already been done, I should like to wish you success in that which you still propose to undertake. I consider that your plans for after the war are not the least important of your activities.—THE RIGHT HON. DAVID LLOYD GEORGE, M.P.

THE Red Triangle is often to be found in unexpected places. ' A wonderful, friendly old octopus, this Y.M.C.A,' was the way an Australian put it, and it was not at all a bad description of the ubiquitous Red Triangle. Tommy recognises it to-day as his club, his meeting house, his home from home. It is his, and he knows it ! It touches him at every point and in almost every place. The recruit finds it at his depôt, near his billet, and in the training camp where he learns to be a soldier ; indeed, it is part of the training, and an important part, too. Passing through London or a great provincial city, he can stay the night in one of the Y.M.C.A. hostels ; he meets it again at the English ports before he embarks for one of the fighting fronts ; it is there to greet him on the other side, not only at the ports of entry and in the base camps, but on the lines of communication in France, Italy, Egypt, Palestine, Mesopotamia, and right up the line, in cellar or dug-out as well as in rest-camp and at railhead. If he should have the misfortune to be wounded he may expect to find the Association at the casualty clearing station or in the hospital, and later on in the convalescent camp, or, if invalided out of the army, it will still stick to him and befriend him at a time when he is likely to need a friend. If he is numbered amongst the missing and finds himself in a prisoner of war camp in Germany, even then he may not be beyond the outreach of the Association. There is at least one redeeming feature to the prisoner of war camp in Ruhleben in Germany, for right in the heart of it there is a little brown hut with the Red Triangle and the letters ' Y.M.C.A.' on the roof—one of several in Germany erected with American Y.M.C.A. money, at a time when America was a neutral state, and run entirely by British prisoners of war for the benefit of their fellow-Britishers, who also have the misfortune to be prisoners of war.

It is little we can do for these brave lads who are wearing their hearts out longing to hear the voices of those they love in the Homeland, but the Y.M.C.A. does what it can.

This girdle of loving-kindness is completed in the Internment Camps of Switzerland — at Mürren, Leysin, Interlaken, Meiringen, and Seeburg, and in those of Holland at Scheveningen, Rotterdam, The Hague, and Groningen. None need our help more than the officers and men of those internment camps. It was one of the latter who said he would rather be in Germany than in the internment camp in Switzerland, for in Germany, said he, one has, at any rate, the excitement of trying to escape; but now, working hand-in-hand with the British Red Cross, the Red Triangle provides recreation and employment for the long hours of leisure, and there can be no doubt as to the appreciation of those it seeks to serve.

A worker at Cambridge went to a neighbouring village to arrange a flag day on behalf of our war fund. He was advised to get in touch with the postmistress, who was keenly interested in the movement. 'Of course, I am interested,' she said when he saw her, 'and if you will come into my sitting-room I will show you why.' There on the wall in a little room at the back of the post-office was what she called her Roll of Honour—the photographs of twelve lads from her Bible class, all serving with His Majesty's Forces. 'Eleven out of the twelve,' said she, 'write me almost every week, and tell me what a boon the Y.M.C.A. is to them. That is why I am ready to do all I can to help you with your Flag Day.' The sequel was interesting. Half an hour later No. 12 called to see her. 'How strange,' she cried; 'I was just talking about you, and saying you were the only one of the boys who never wrote express-ing appreciation of the Y.M.C.A.' 'That is easily explained,' was the reply. 'I have been at sea since the early days of the war, and have had no opportunity of getting ashore and using the Y.M.C.A. until three months ago, when I was sent to Egypt and stationed at the Mena camp. There I used the Association hut within sight of the great pyramid, and I appreciate the work as much as anyone to-day.'

A young soldier who was formerly a Y.M.C.A. worker wrote from France :— ' We came upon the Prussian Guard about ten days ago, and for five days and nights we fought hand to hand like demons, but in the end we gained our objective. You talk of the work of the Y.M.C.A. at home as splendid. I know it is, but here the Y.M.C.A.'s are more. In this place, famous for its wonderful bell tower, the Y.M.C.A. is in full swing, although only yesterday it was shelled heavily and shrapnel was falling pretty thick along the road. Cheero ! ' Another young soldier wrote from Malta, and gave his experience of the Y.M.C.A. 'The Association is the finest thing that was ever instituted without doubt. The Army has blessed the fact many a time. I have served in France and a few other countries, and am in a position to know.'

In the early days of the war Y.M.C.A. secretaries learned to adapt all kinds of premises, no matter how primitive, to meet the needs of the troops. A cow-house amid the trenches of the East Coast; a pigsty in the south-west of England, neither of them much to look at, but doing good service and helping to blaze the trail; a dug-out at Anzac and three tiny marquees at Cape Helles; a cellar at Meroc, just behind the British lines in the neighbourhood of Loos; a château formerly the residence of the lord of the manor at Mazingarbe, and a palatial but ruined Technical Institute at Armentières. It was fixed up in a convent at Aire —the first Y.M.C.A. to be opened in a forward position in France, and inside a ruined hospice at Ypres ; in a Trappist monastery on the Mont des Cats ; in the most southern city in the world at Invercargill ; above the clouds with the British troops in Italy ; inside some of the German prisoner of war camps in Germany ; in the old German Consulate at Jaffa, in the heart of the Holy City, and on the Palestine lines of communication at Gaza and Beersheba. 'The Jolly Farmer' near Aldershot, and the more notorious ' Bolger's ' public house in' Sackville Street, Dublin, made their appearance early in the war under the sign of the Red Triangle, whilst Ciro's, the once famous night club in the heart of ' London, and the mansions of Viscount Wimborne and Lord Brassey have also been thrown open for the service of the Association.

The trail of the Red Triangle was first blazed in the United Kingdom, and since then it has become familiar on every fighting front, and in all sorts of queer and unexpected places: in the jungle of India; on the banks of the Tigris, the Euphrates, and the Nile; amid the swamps of East Africa; along the valley of the Jordan; in the Egyptian desert; in the great training camps of North America; in Australasia and South Africa, as well as in the plains of Flanders and Picardy; in the valleys of the Somme, the Marne, the Meuse, and the Aisne. It is to be found on the Varda and the Struma, and we have seen for ourselves how that trail has been welcomed by men of many nationalities—Britons from the Homeland and from the outposts of Empire, from Canada, Newfoundland, Australia, New Zealand, and South Africa; Indians, Chinese, Cape Boys and Kaffirs, Frenchmen, Portuguese, and Belgians, and wherever the trail of the Red Triangle goes it stands for reconstruction even amid the horrors and desolation of war.

An officer cadet who had spent two years in France, said he had noticed a great change in the attitude of the men. 'In the early days of the war,' said he, 'men on arriving in new billets at the Front would say, "Is there no Y.M.C.A. in the village?" Later on they took it for granted that the Red Triangle was there and asked, "Where is the Y.M.C.A.?" Now they always say, "Where is it?" and every one knows to what they refer.' It brings comfort, hope, good cheer, and inspiration with it. An English boy writing home from Egypt to his people in the Midlands, said that the Y.M.C.A. was to him as 'a bit of Heaven in a world that was otherwise all hell.' A visitor to the Association at Kantara expressed his surprise at finding such a splendid Y.M.C.A. building in that Egyptian centre, fitted up even with hot and cold baths !

A sum of £400 was taken in a single day over the refreshment counter in one of the Y.M.C.A. marquees in the heart of the Sinai Peninsula, and it will give an idea of the immense amount of work involved to the staff of the Association, when it is remembered that all stores had to be conveyed from the railhead to the Y.M.C.A. on the backs of camels.

A British soldier writing from the ' Adam and Eve ' hut in Mesopotamia said, ' I should like to comment upon the wonderful work the Y.M.C.A. is doing here among the troops. In almost every large camp there is a Y.M.C.A. hut, a veritable haven in the desert, not only for canteen, but religious work also. I attended a service in the hut, and it made a good impression on me. We sang the good old hymns, and I am sure we all felt refreshed.'

As might be expected, the Dominions have done their full share of pioneering, and have blazed the trail in many different directions. The Canadians have done a great work at Shorncliffe, Sandling, Bramshott, and Witley ; in the Forestry camps at home and right up the line in France. The Australians on Salisbury Plain, at Weymouth, and in many other home centres have served their troops splendidly; whilst in France, Egypt, the Dardanelles, and Palestine their pioneering work has been great. The New Zealanders at Sling Plantation, Hornchurch, and other centres at home, have done equally well, and their pioneering work overseas has been most efficient. The South Africans have done valuable work in the Military Expedition to Swakopmund and in East Africa. India has made a great contribution to the

Empire work of the Red Triangle, first of all by catering for the needs of British troops quartered in India itself, and also in Mesopotamia and East Africa, where the work has been directed from India, as has that for the Indian troops in France. Passing reference should also be made here to the great programme of work undertaken and planned by the Y.M.C.A.'s of the United States. In the United Kingdom, in France, Russia and Italy, as well as in North America, they have projected work on an enormous scale, in fact, all the Allied countries are closely cooperating in the work of the Red Triangle. It has been the privilege of the British Associations to provide huts for the exclusive use of Belgian, Serbian, and Portuguese troops, and to cater for the needs of American and Colonial soldiers in hundreds of centres. In London, for instance, special facilities have been given to New Zealanders at the Shakespeare hut ; we were able to procure for the Canadian Y.M.C.A. the magnificent Tivoli site on which their fine hostel now stands, and to hand over the group of huts to the Americans which formed the nucleus of the Eagle Hut. The Australians rented and furnished the Aldwych Theatre on their own account. The New Zealand Y.M.C.A.'s made a handsome contribution towards the cost of the Shakespeare Hut, and the whole of the cost of the Eagle and Beaver Huts has been borne by the American and Canadian Y.M.C.A.'s, respectively. The American and Colonial Associations have taken over a number of British huts in camps, and in some cases have enlarged them.

THE FIRST Y.M.C.A. OVER THE GERMAN TRENCHES ON THE SOMME BATTLEFIELD

THE Y.M.C.A. IN THE ORCHARD AT ALBERT

CHAPTER III

FLOTSAM AND JETSAM

In my opinion nothing can exceed the value of the work which has been and is being done for H.M. Forces by the Y.M.C.A. I offer my best wishes for continued success.—THE RIGHT HON. H. H. ASQUITH, K.C., M.P.

THE Romance of the Red Triangle is a twenty-four hours a day romance, for many of its centres never close their doors. When we are comfortably sleeping at night and in the early hours of the morning, Y.M.C.A. workers are hard at work on motor patrol conveying leave men from station to station or hut to hut, and others are on foot meeting the men and guiding them to their destination. Alighting from the Edinburgh train at Leeds very early one morning, it was raining and a young Scottish trooper stepped down to the platform from the adjoining compartment. We knew we were all right, a room having been retained for us at the Station Hotel; but what of him? Had he anywhere to go? He evidently had no plans, but at that moment a gentleman in civilian attire stepped up to him, and without patronising, and in the most natural way possible said to him, 'Have you long to wait? Have you anywhere to go?' The lad replied that he had several hours to wait for his connection and had nowhere to go. 'Well, come along with me, and I will see you all right at the Y.M.C.A.' People who do this work or devote themselves, night after night, to that of the motor patrols don't often get their photos into the papers, but they are rendering national service of a high order without fee or reward, and in almost every case, at the end of a hard day's work.

The International Hospitality League of the Y.M.C.A. is doing similar work on a very large scale, and in its kiosks and inquiry rooms, not only in London, but in Glasgow, Edinburgh, and many of our large provincial centres hundreds of thousands of inquiries are being received and answered day by day, whilst the street patrol workers have been able to help very many who have welcomed their assistance.

We know of no more moving sight than one of the great Triage huts in France when leave is on. We think of our last visit to one such. Three hundred men were sleeping there that night, and 'Uncle Joe,' the Y.M.C.A. leader, went round the bunks last thing to see them safely tucked in. As we stood in the main hall we thought we understood what was said of our Lord that ' when He saw the multitude He was filled with compassion.' Scores of men were gathered around the piano, singing rowdy choruses of the kind loved by our Tommies. The coffee queue extended the whole length of the room, and the men had to buy their tickets from Uncle Joe, who had a few words with each in homely Lancashire dialect, whilst further along the counter a titled lady was serving coffee as fast as she could pour it out. There were crowds round the tables, reading or feeding. We noticed at one table a group of men, one of whom was cutting up a long French loaf, another had just opened a tin of sardines which he was sharing round, whilst a third was helping his comrades from a tin of pears. All were on their way home on leave, or returning to the Front, and all were merry and happy as British Tommies almost invariably are.

Sometimes in a London hut, or it may be in the Y.M.C.A. in Paris, you will come across one of these Tommies who is down and out. He has been on leave and has spent or lost all his money, and is down on his luck. It is to the Y.M.C.A. he turns. A little act of kindness, under such circumstances, has often changed a man's whole outlook on life. Nearly the whole of the service in the Y.M.C.A. hostels is rendered voluntarily, and many workers who have home or business ties welcome this opportunity of doing war service that really counts. There is a tendency in some quarters to speak disparagingly of the voluntary worker, but those who know, realise the enormous value of such service. No paid workers could have been more zealous or more efficient than those who have served voluntarily under the Red Triangle. The old brewery in Earl Street was the first building in London to be adapted for sleeping purposes, but the 'Euston' was the first Y.M.C.A.

hostel to be built.   One of the largest is the Shakespeare Hut which was built on the site of the proposed National Shakespeare Memorial Theatre, kindly loaned for the purpose.   The huge building by London Bridge was lent by the city of London.   Many of the huts occupy central and important sites, as for instance, the station huts at King's Cross, Victoria, and Waterloo,—and the station hut often means the last touch of home before men go overseas, and that makes the work and the personality of the workers all the more important.

CHAPTER IV

THE ROMANCE OF FINANCE

This work has been admirably done both at home
and at the Front. Its spiritual and material value
to the men lies beyond all reckoning, and the
services of its personnel are deeply appreciated by
the men themselves.—THE RIGHT HON. A. J.
BALFOUR, O.M., M.P.

ON August 4, 1914, our plan for war work
was ready, but the 'sinews of war' were
lacking. Little could be done without
money. In our extremity we laid the
whole position before one of our most
generous leaders and supporters, and told
him of the opportunity we saw facing the
Y.M.C.A. 'If we are to seize the opportunity,' we said, 'it is absolutely necesary
we should secure immediately twenty-five
thousand pounds!' He looked up and
smiled indulgently—'Twenty-five thou-

sand pounds!' he cried; 'you couldn't possibly raise three thousand pounds at a time like this; the thing's impossible!' 'Impossible or not,' was the reply, 'it must be done. We mustn't even stop to think of the future of the Y.M.C.A. Everything is at stake, and even if we have to sell every building and every stick of furniture we possess we must go forward now!' That very day a large number of telegrams and letters were sent out from Headquarters to friends all over the country—the first war emergency appeal of the Red Triangle —and within a few days the whole of the twenty-five thousand pounds had been raised, and we were appealing for another fifty thousand pounds, until at the time of writing, in August 1918, the war fund has reached the total of nearly two and a half millions sterling. That is a small sum compared with the amounts raised for Y.M.C.A. war work in the United States.

Their first appeal brought in five million pounds, the second more than twelve millions, and their appeal a year later, in October 1918, is for twenty millions sterling. Our American friends gave us a hundred thousand pounds from the amount raised by their second war work appeal, a generous and much appreciated gift. People who know little of the facts are sometimes inclined to criticise what they regard as the huge war expenditure of the British Y.M.C.A.'s, but a moment's reflection will make it clear that it has been little short of a miracle of finance to carry out such an enormous programme of work at a total cost of only about one-third of the cost to Britain alone of a single day of war. We have always been short of money, have always had a big overdraft at the bank, and that largely because we have had to finance a huge business concern without capital. Our war fund has been secured partly as a result of skilful advertising, partly through personal solicitation and in response to postal appeals. Flag Days and Hut Weeks also proved valuable agencies for raising money. The full-page Y.M.C.A. advertisements in *The Times* and other papers were something quite new in religious and social work advertising, though the method has since been widely adopted by other organisations.

Many touching stories are told concerning gifts to the war fund, gifts, many of which have not been secured as a result of cleverly drawn advertisements, but because the contributors have been touched directly or indirectly by the work itself. A boy wrote home from Flanders, 'Tell Dad if he has any money to spare to give it to the Y.M.C.A. as a thankoffering for what they are doing for us chaps out here.' One of our centres had been nearly destroyed by a Zeppelin bomb. It was rebuilt and the day came for the reopening. A lady was present and expressed herself thus : ' I wanted to be here to-day, if only to thank you for what your Association has done for my boy. When the war broke out,' said she, ' he went to the Crystal Palace for his training, and found the Y.M.C.A. there an inestimable boon. He was sent to Blandford to complete his training, and the Y.M.C.A. was there. He was drafted out to Gallipoli, and to his amazement he found the Y.M.C.A. on the Peninsula. He was wounded and sent to Suez, where once more the Y.M.C.A. was a great help to him, and yesterday,' she continued, ' I received a letter from him from Alexandria saying he was convalescent, and spending the whole of his spare time in the central building of the Association.' It is that personal touch that has made the appeal of the Red

Triangle one of the most popular appeals of the war.

A lady called one day with a novel suggestion. She had been reading a statement attributed to the Kaiser, in which the All Highest is alleged to have said that if the worst came to the worst every dog and cat in Germany would be armed in defence of the Fatherland. ' If the dogs and cats of Germany are going to do that for their country,' she said, ' why shouldn't the dogs and cats of England pay for one of your huts ? ' Quite frankly there did not appear to be much money in the scheme, but it could do no harm, so we encouraged it ! Imagine our surprise when a few days later the same lady walked in with a cheque for four hundred and fifty pounds. There was one gift of five pounds, all the rest had been given in smaller amounts, and altogether upwards of two thousand dogs and cats—or their masters and mistresses—had contributed. A few weeks later the fund was closed, at just over one thousand pounds, and there has been no more useful centre of Y.M.C.A. war work than the 'Dogs and Cats Hut' at Roucn, paid for entirely by this fund.

The Boys and Girls fund has reached upwards of twenty thousand pounds. We had been speaking to the boys at Harrow School, and the suggestion had been thrown out that it would be a good plan to have a 'Harrow' Hut at the Front. At the close of the meeting the headmaster, supporting the suggestion, said he would give the collection in chapel the following Sunday to the fund. The head boy approached him afterwards and said, 'I think, Sir, it would be a mistake to make a collection for the Y.M.C.A. on Sunday. If you do the boys will think they have done their bit, and won't bother any further. Won't you let us make a whip

up round the houses and see what we can
do ? ' Thus it was agreed, and the five
hundred pounds, which in those days was
the cost of a hut, was raised in less than a
week. We have seen that hut in France,
and know how much it was appreciated.
During the German advance in Picardy it
had to be temporarily abandoned, but
fortunately was speedily occupied again.

In the early days of the Euston hut,
the vicar of a neighbouring parish was
keenly interested, and told the children in
his day school what he had seen in the hut.
At the close of his address a deputation
of the older children waited on him and
told him they were interested in what he
told them, and would much like to help
the Y.M.C.A. in its work for the soldiers.
' You help ? ' queried the vicar ; ' how
can you help ? ' He knew how poor they
were. To his surprise they had their
scheme ready, and their plans cut and

dried. 'This time every year,' said the spokesman, 'we put by our pennies and our ha'pennies for our annual treat. We don't feel like having a treat this year when all this terrible fighting is taking place. We would rather give the money to the Y.M.C.A. to spend on the soldiers and sailors.' A few days later, the leader of the Euston hut was sitting at a table in the central hall when his attention was attracted by a group of ragged children, standing round the entrance. Curiously they would peer inside and then step back, until two or three bolder than the others walked right in as if the whole place belonged to them. That was too much for the leader. He went up to them and cried, 'You must run away; this place isn't for boys and girls, it's for soldiers and sailors.' Looking up into his face a little ragged youngster retorted, 'Please, sir, we've given our money towards this show, and we want to see how it's run!' On inquiry, it was ascertained that the children belonged to one of the poorest of the schools in the north of London, and out of their poverty they had given no less than thirty shillings, nearly the whole of it in pennies and farthings. Many memorial gifts have been received, and a hut that will be an inspiration and help to tens of thousands, is surely one of the most suitable of memorials.

Business firms and merchant princes have given their thousands ; others, with equal generosity, have contributed shillings. In the Channel Islands, there was a fish-hawker, named Richards, who eked out a slender livelihood by selling fish on the streets of Jersey. The coming of the war hit him so hard that he was compelled to leave for France to seek other employment. He got a job under the contractors who were building the hutments in the

A REFUGE FOR THE REFUGEES

Y.M.C.A. MARQUEE IN THE SHELL-SWEPT SOMME AREA

Harfleur Valley. He did well, and eventually returned home to Jersey. The Sunday after his return, his minister was taking up special collections for the hut fund. Richards had found the Red Triangle huts at Havre a great boon, and on entering the church at the evening service, handed his minister a little paper packet containing coins. The padre fingered the parcel and said to himself, ' He has given six pennies, a generous gift, too, under the circumstances ! ' Imagine his surprise on opening the packet to find there six half-crowns. He said, ' You ought not to give so much ; you can't possibly afford it.' ' When I remember all the Y.M.C.A. did for me when a stranger in France and homeless,' was his reply, ' I can't possibly do less, and wish I could give more.'

A flower-seller at a popular seaside holiday resort for many months has given to the local Y.M.C.A. hut a shillingsworth of flowers each week, as a thankoffering for what the Association has done for her husband and son.

At Taunton a farm labourer called at the back door of the house of the president of the local Y.M.C.A., and said he wanted to help the war fund. It was the only thing he could do to help the men at the Front. He had tried to enlist several times, but they would not have him. He laid on the table fifty one-pound notes, and went back to his work on the farm. Inquiries elicited the fact that he had given practically the whole of his savings, and had done it in spite of his employer's urgent advice to the contrary.

At the close of a meeting held by one of our workers, an elderly lady came to him and said if he would go to her house she would give him a sovereign. He went, and she gave him the coin, and then closing the door of her private room, said, ' And now I am going to give you the most precious possession I have in the world.' Her voice choked with emotion as she proceeded, ' Years, many years ago, I was to have been married. The arrangements were made, the day fixed, and the ring bought, and—*then he died*!' And she sobbed as she spoke. Going to a bureau she took out a little box and, handing it to him, said, ' The wedding ring is in there. I have kept it all these years, but I promised the Lord I would only keep it until He showed me what He would have me do with it, and He told me while you were speaking. I give it to you for the Y.M.C.A. and for the boys,' and she turned away utterly broken up. Thousands of incidents could be related of equal interest to the foregoing, did space permit, and all these incidents combine to give a personal interest to the fund.

We can only add that the greatest possible care has been taken to administer the fund wisely and so avoid waste, or anything that savours of extravagance. Of course, Y.M.C.A. finance has come in for criticism. Certain people who have visited the huts, and have seen the enormous business there transacted have come to the conclusion that either very large profits are being made, or that the business methods of the Association leave much to be desired. The question has frequently been asked, ' What is done with the profits ? ' and the fiction has got abroad that the Y.M.C.A. publishes no accounts and is amassing huge sums of money. The real position is easily stated :—

The Y.M.C.A. does not do trading for trading's sake, but because through its trading department it is the better enabled to meet the needs of the troops, and also because profits on trading mean further extension. So rapid has been the development of the war work of the Y.M.C.A., that not only has every penny of profit been spent on the maintenance and development of this work for soldiers and sailors, but it has been necessary to raise large sums of money in subscriptions to meet the ever-increasing demand for extension. Every new centre means, or may mean, an additional burden on the central fund or on the divisional funds for which the National Council is ultimately responsible. First, there is the cost of the hut, which may mean £750 or may run into thousands—it all depends upon size and site. The initial cost may be defrayed by an individual gift to the central war fund, but usually to make the hut large enough for its purpose, additional money has to be spent,

whilst the furnishing will probably cost
from one to three hundred pounds, or
more. Also, it must carry stock to
the value of a hundred pounds or
possibly much more if it is a big camp.
A very big turnover in a Triangle hut
may represent a very small profit, *e.g.*
there are enormous sales of stamps and
postal orders, and all these are sold for
actual cost, and, what is more, the
Association has to bear the loss of
shortages. Then there are the things
the Y.M.C.A. does free of any charges
whatever, *e.g.* there are no club fees
and no charges for admission to concerts, lectures, or entertainments in the
ordinary hut. Free writing paper and
envelopes are at the present time cost-
ing more than £90,000 a year. Thousands of pounds are spent on cricket
and football outfits, games generally,
books, pictures, and literature for free

distribution. Hot drinks and refreshments are given free to the walking wounded on a very large scale, and practically every one of the two thousand war Y.M.C.A.'s keeps 'open house' at Christmas. The work of the Y.M.C.A. for the relatives of wounded is very costly, especially in France, many hostels being maintained for that purpose. Motor transport is an expensive item for which there is no return, and very large sums of money are spent on lectures and educational work. It is estimated that the Y.M.C.A. educational programme in France alone may ultimately cost the Association fifty thousand pounds a year. When the request has come to open a new centre, the determining factor has been, 'Is it needed?' not 'Will it pay?' Indeed many huts in isolated centres cannot possibly be made to pay, and yet they mean everything to the men who use them. The spending department of the Association has been built up with the greatest care. A body of well-known business men meets for hours every week and watches expenditure as a cat watches a mouse. The Acting Treasurer of the War Emergency Fund is a partner in a big firm of Indian Merchants, and devotes himself with untiring energy and conspicuous ability to the supervision of accounts and to the expenditure. The accounts are audited by a leading firm of chartered accountants, and the audited statement of receipts and expenditure together with a balance sheet, is published in *The Times* and other papers every six months. In the canteens it is a matter of principle to give full value for money spent, but towards the war services the profits made have been equal to a sum of ten shillings for every pound contributed by the public. Owing chiefly to the enormous stores that have to be maintained in France and Overseas generally, the Bank overdraft of the war fund has often reached four and five hundred thousand pounds. It is thus not difficult to see what is done with the profits. The Y.M.C.A. might, had it so chosen, have feathered its nest during the war, but with a sublime, though by no means a reckless disregard of the future it stepped right into the breach, and went straight forward to meet the national need.

As a Y.M.C.A. we pride ourselves on the business management of our work. We insist on business methods being adopted, and we do not mix our business with philanthropy—the Association hut is not a charity as far as its business side

is concerned. The average hut in a large
camp is expected to pay its way, so that
subscriptions from the general public can
 e applied to the extension of the work
ind to the maintenance of centres that
cannot be self-supporting.

The War Office, in the early stages of
the war, asked us to pay a rebate of
10 per cent. on the gross takings of the
refreshment department. After full consideration, we came to the conclusion that
we could only do this by extracting the
money from the pockets of the men, who
for the most part are miserably paid, by
paying it out of subscriptions given by the
public, or by limiting the extension of the
work. Neither alternative seemed desir-
able or in the interests of the men, and after
many conferences with the Quartermaster-
General's department at the War Office, it
was agreed, by mutual consent and at the
suggestion of the War Office, to refer the

matter for decision to the Secretary of
State for War. It was at the time Lord
Kitchener was in Gallipoli, and Mr. Asquith
was personally in charge. At a conference
at Downing Street the representatives of
the Board of Control Regimental Institutes
stated their case, and we had the opportunity of replying. Mr. Asquith took
several weeks to consider the question in
all its bearings, and ultimately gave the
decision entirely in our favour, and decided
for the duration of the war we should not
be asked to pay the rebate. Later on,
the matter was reopened by Lord Derby,
and eventually it was found necessary
for the Y.M.C.A. to pay 6 per cent. on
their gross takings in huts on Military
ground, to regimental funds, and this
is a great tax on its resources. Most
of the huts are loaned free to the
Military for church parades and military
lectures.

The figures of the Red Triangle are colossal, and yet figures by themselves fail to give an adequate idea of the magnitude of the work, and for obvious reasons it is impossible to make those statistics complete. On a given date it was ascertained that upwards of forty-five thousand workers were giving regular service to the war work of the Y.M.C.A. By August 31, 1918, 929,590,430 pieces of stationery had been sent out from Y.M.C.A. Headquarters in London for distribution amongst the men of His Majesty's Forces. The stationery bill by the summer of 1918 had risen to the rate of upwards of £90,000 per annum.

In two months one hundred and five tents were sent out to replace the huts and tents lost in Picardy and Flanders.

In eighteen months, Triangle House, London, the Headquarters of our Trading

Department, sent out: to the Y.M.C.A. overseas :—

875 Gramophones and 8386 Records.
322 Pianos and Organs.
572 Billiard and Bagatelle Tables.
1,341 Sets of Boxing Gloves.
108 Optical Lanterns.
10,188 Sets of Draughts.
1,335 Sets of Chess.
3,140 Sets of Dominoes.
4,263 Footballs.
1,080 Sets of Quoits.
657 Sets of Cricket.
4,992 Extra Balls.
1,540 Extra Bats.
1,798 Hockey Sticks.
520 Balls.
426 Golf Balls.
100 Tennis Sets.
330 Tennis Racquets.
2,364 Tennis Balls.
61 Sets Bowls.
358 Badminton Sets.
50 Baseball Sets.

It will be noted that the items in this list are not trading goods to be sold at a profit, but excepting in the case of some of the billiard tables, are non-remunerative, and provided absolutely free for the use of the men serving overseas.

CHAPTER V

THE LADIES OF THE RED TRIANGLE

I have received Her Majesty's commands to convey
to you an expression of the Queen's sincere thanks
for the interesting information you have given
regarding the work which is being done by the
Young Men's Christian Association among the men
of the Army and Navy.

Her Majesty is much pleased with the specimens
of writing-papers and envelopes, and publications,
which you have sent for her acceptance.

Her Majesty feels sure that the useful work which
is being carried on by the Young Men's Christian
Association in so many different centres is highly
appreciated not only by the soldiers, but also by
the community.—HER MAJESTY THE QUEEN.

BEFORE the war it was one of our stock
sayings that the Y.M.C.A. was a work
'for young men by young men,' and one
must recognise the fact that the man who
is a *man*—virile, strong, athletic—is the
one to whose leadership men will most
readily respond. But in the early days

of the war most of our young male workers
joined up; whether we liked it or not we
had to get the help of ladies, and our
more enterprising leaders felt that after
all there were some things in Y.M.C.A.
hut work ladies could do almost as well
as men. Things have moved since then,
and now we know that much of the work
can be done infinitely better by women.
In many cases women have been entrusted
with the actual leadership of huts, and have
carried through the duties magnificently.
The Red Triangle has given the woman
her niche in the Y.M.C.A., and for the
great programme that awaits us after the
war her help will be indispensable. It
has, moreover, given the woman who had
home claims an opportunity of doing war
work that really counts, in her spare time.
The Queen and Queen Alexandra have
been graciously interested in the work of
the ladies of the Red Triangle, and many

Y.M.C.A. IN A RUINED PARISH HALL IN FLANDERS, JUNE, 1916

BAPAUME-CAMBRAI ROAD, WITH TREES ALL CUT DOWN BY THE GERMANS

of the ladies of the Royal House have rendered conspicuous personal service, amongst whom might be mentioned H.R.H. Princess Christian, H.R.H. Princess Louise, H.R.H. Princess Patricia of Connaught, and H.H. Princess Marie Louise, whilst H.H. Princess Helena Victoria as Lady President has given time and strength to the work without reserve, and we owe very much to her. In the camps, ladies have given the home touch that means so much to the men—games, music, decorations, and flowers have come within their domain ; they have managed the libraries, and have in most cases taken full responsibility for the refreshment department. Their personal influence has been invaluable. We remember visiting a camp somewhere in France. It seemed to us the roughest camp we had ever seen. The leader told us of an encounter he had with one of the worst of the men on the occa-

E

sion of his first visit to the place. He had just got his tent erected, and the man chancing to see it asked what it was. When told that it was the Y.M.C.A., he replied, ' You b—— men are just what we d—— men b—— well want,' and that was the language of the camp. Eighteen months later we were there again and the camp was like another place, so great was the change for the better. The C.O. told us he attributed that change almost entirely to the ladies of the Red Triangle. It so happened that one of the ladies committed an unpardonable military offence. She returned to England two or three days before her permit expired. Later on, application was made in the usual way for the renewal of her permit. The General concerned, who is no longer in France,. returned the application with the words written across it over his initials—' Keep this woman out.' The Base Commandant

sent it in again having written on it—
'Talk about keeping this woman out, she
is of more value to me than truckloads of
parsons and chaplains!' That was his
way of putting it, not ours. We have the
greatest possible admiration for the work
of the chaplains at the Front. There is no
finer body of men on active service to-day,
and it is a privilege we greatly esteem to be
permitted to co-operate with them and to be
of some service to them in their great work.

The ladies have always been ready to
share the risks with the men, and there
are quite a number who have made the
supreme sacrifice, including Miss Smallpage,
killed by shrapnel in one of our munition
huts in England ; Miss Betty Stevenson,
killed in an air attack in France ; Miss
Edith Howe, who died of cerebro-spinal
meningitis ; and Miss Lee, who lost her
life in a fire in one of the huts on Salisbury
Plain.

In one of the great bases in France there is a small camp in which at one time there were boys only. They were too young to fight, their job day by day was the prosaic one of filling up petrol cans. One of these little chaps had badly hurt his hand, and it seemed to him the natural thing to go for sympathy and help to the lady of the Red Triangle. A brief examination convinced her that the damage was serious, and she bade him go to the doctor, whose tent was just across the way. Very grudgingly he trudged across to the doctor, but a few minutes later returned with the request that she would look at the damaged hand and see if the doctor had attended to it properly. She replied that it would never do to interfere with the doctor's work and, moreover, the doctor had no doubt done it far better than she could have done. Five times the lad came back with the request, ' O Missis ! do look at my hand

and see if he 's done it right.' The fifth time he brought with him as an ally the Y.M.C.A. secretary in charge, who said, ' If I were you, Miss, I would look at his hand. The little chap will never be happy until you do.' Then she undid the bandages, looked at the dressing, and bandaging it up again said, ' There, it 's just as I told you ; the doctor has done it far better than I could ; run away and be quite happy about it ! ' He went away, but returned again a few minutes later, and that time his eyes were full of tears as he cried, ' O Missis ! I did think you 'd have kissed me when you saw how bad it was,' and, like the good woman she was, she kissed him as his mother would have done. Let no one think that 's what the ladies of the Red Triangle usually do, for it 's not, and yet in that simple story you have the whole secret of the success of the war work of the Y.M.C.A. Time, and time

again, one has been through every base
camp in France, and has traversed the
whole British line in France and Flanders,
and wherever one has gone one has found
the men yearning for sympathy and
longing for home. Not that they want
to return home until this fight ends in
victory, for out there they have learned
what war means ; they see it robbed of its
romance, and they are determined to see
it through ; they fight that this war may
end war.

With unfailing loyalty to the high aims
of the Red Triangle and with conspicuous
ability ladies have served the Y.M.C.A.,
and through the Association the men of
His Majesty's Forces and the munition
workers, in all parts of the United Kingdom,
in France, and in every part of the Empire,
and have won for themselves a permanent
place in the movement, whatever its future
may be.

CHAPTER VI

'GUNGA DIN' OF THE RED TRIANGLE

'You and your Association seem to me to be truly hitting the nail on the head, and working for the good of our soldier-lads, one and all. I have watched the Y.M.C.A. procedure at many camps, and have found it exactly adapted to the wants of large numbers of young men taken temporarily away from their homes and normal associations.'—GENERAL SIR IAN HAMILTON.

ONE of the most striking of Kipling's characters was Gunga Din, the Indian water-carrier. He was not a fighting man, but when fighting was taking place he was in the thick of it, risking his life that he might carry water to slake the thirst of the fighting man. 'Gunga Din' was the appropriate name given to one of our leaders in France by a British Tommy. Those who do not know are sometimes inclined to sneer at the Y.M.C.A. man for having a ' cushy ' job, but it is hard work from start to finish. His job is never done and very often is attended with considerable risk. His work may carry him right into the front line trenches and though it does not take him ' over the top,' yet, unlike the soldier, he has not the privilege of hitting back. His day's work will vary according to the camp. In all probability he will have to be up early in the morning, to get the coffee ready. The hut must be cleaned, and there will be a lot of canteen work to be done. The buying will occupy some time, and then there will be the evening programme to arrange and carry through. He must maintain personal touch with the men using the hut, so that the ideal leader must be half a dozen men rolled into one.

Our greatest difficulty during the war has been that of getting a sufficiency of workers of the right type. Every male

worker is registered with the Director of
Recruiting, and we are unable to recruit
new men classified A between the ages of
18 and 52, or 18 and 45 for service overseas.

Twelve members of the Y.M.C.A. have
won the Victoria Cross, 3 the D.S.O.,
33 the M.C., 25 the D.C.M., and 53 the M.M.,
whilst registered at Headquarters are the
names of 1223 who have made the supreme
sacrifice. We think of many whose war
work for the Y.M.C.A. has earned the title
of ' Gunga Din,' as, for example, the young
leader of the New Zealand work in France.
He looks a boy, but is a genius for organising, and the pioneer of the work of the Red
Triangle in advanced positions. Another
man who has the instincts of the pioneer is
the leader of the Australian workers in
Egypt and Palestine, and yet another, a
well-known Y.M.C.A. worker who, after
doing good service in England in the
early days of the war, went to represent

Headquarters in Egypt. Torpedoed *en route* he took up his new work with characteristic enthusiasm and made good. Hundreds have rendered equally valuable service, so that it would be invidious to mention names.

In the great retreat, it was the D.A.Q.M.G. of the — Corps who asked us to open up a Stragglers' Post at Westoutre. ' You are the people who can cheer up the men,' said he ; 'I want you to get hold of the stragglers before they become deserters.' It was ' Gunga Din ' he needed, but this time with cocoa-urn instead of water-bottle, and it was only an old bank to which our workers fixed their Red Triangle, but it was just what was needed. A bursting shell forced them to quit, but half an hour later they had opened up again in the village shop, opposite the church, and the mayor thanked them later on for their successful efforts.

Our officers' hut at Romerin was set on
fire by a shell; shells were falling fast,
and the larger hut soon became untenable,
but the Y.M.C.A. man was running his show
in the open under a tree, and was as busy
as ever. The ubiquitous 'Ford' did its
bit, and its load would sometimes consist
of the Divisional Secretary himself, one or
two other workers or Belgian refugees, a
big caterer's boiler, a tea-urn, together with
cases of biscuits and cigarettes. Thus
equipped, it would proceed to some
advanced dressing - station. Sometimes
there would only be a sergeant and orderlies
in charge, heroically doing their best to
help the wounded, and the mere presence
of a man like one of our secretaries gave
them confidence, whilst the steaming hot
drinks he soon had ready gave new courage
to the wounded men who thronged the
C.C.S. A great work of the 'Gunga Din'
type was [done on the Nieppe - Bailleul

road during the retreat. What an amazing scene it must have been ; an endless stream of refugees and wounded ; units lost ; batteries firing ; men who had been for days without food, moving about like ghosts and digging themselves in at the side of the road. The Huns were only about eight hundred yards further along the road, and our soldiers fired as they walked. For three nights none of our workers even thought of going to bed ; they stood by with cars ready to help where and how they were most needed, and gave help to soldiers and refugees alike. At dressing and casualty clearing stations they gave emergency help. At Remy, for instance, one of our men was told off to undress the wounded and rig them out - in new pyjamas, whilst another made himself useful in cleaning the floors. Hot drinks were given out freely in all these centres just behind the line.

Following the British victory at Messines on June 7, 1917, a Leeds minister serving on the staff of the Y.M.C.A. wrote home describing the work for the walking wounded as he had seen it :—

'It was about three o'clock in the morning when the signal to advance was given, and the boys went over the parapet. About two hours later the wounded began to arrive at our hospital in ambulance vans. It had been previously arranged that only as far as possible walking cases—men slightly wounded—should be dealt with at our station, and the expeditious and efficient way in which their wounds were attended to reflected great credit on the medical staff. As soon as they left the dressing-room they were passed on to our Y.M.C.A., where we supplied them with various kinds of refreshments free. It was my great privilege to serve the first patient, who had a broken arm, with a freshly-made cup of tea and a sandwich, and never shall I forget his look and words of appreciation. Some were too ill to eat anything for a time, especially those who had been gassed or were suffering from shell-shock, but they were very glad of a seat on the grass in the shade of our tent. Some were so badly wounded that they were unable to speak, while others were half deaf and dumb as the result of shock. It was pathetic to see such men scribbling their request for a drink on a piece of paper. All were loud in their praise of the Y.M.C.A. and many were quite overcome when they realised that the tea, lemonade, cigarettes, and various kinds of eatables were provided free. One Scottish New Zealander, whose father is a well-known seed merchant in Edinburgh, declared

that the Y.M.C.A. was the greatest
thing in the war. In addition to
attending to the needs of the " inner
man "—and some of them we had to
feed like babies, as both hands were
wounded—we wrote letters and field
cards for them, and tried in every
possible way to add to their comfort.
The spirit manifested by the majority
of them was simply splendid, and
scarcely ever did they refer to their
own suffering and hardships.'

CHAPTER VII

IN THE TRAIL OF THE HUN

It has given me great pleasure to learn of the development of the Y.M.C.A. work in France and England during the last six months. In particular I am very glad to hear of the successful growth of the experiment begun at Aire.

No one can be long in this country without realising the immense value of your organisation, and the constant extension of your activities itself testifies to the high regard in which it is held by our soldiers.—FIELD-MARSHAL SIR DOUGLAS HAIG.

THE history of the British Empire has been written over again, and written in blood, in the valleys of the Somme, the Ancre, and the Scarpe. Tens of thousands of our noblest and best lie buried in these valleys or on the tableland of Peronne, situated between the insignificant rivers that have within the past few months earned a world-wide notoriety. No one can visit a modern battlefield without

THE RED TRIANGLE IN THE SUPPORT TRENCHES

'GEORGE WILLIAMS HOUSE' IN THE FRONT TRENCHES

A HALF-WAY HOUSE TO THE TRENCHES

realising something of the appalling waste of war. Towns and villages have been blotted out of existence, or are marked to-day by a few unrecognisable ruins. Thanks to the efficiency of British organisation, excellent roads were quickly established right through the stricken district, and it was impossible to traverse any of them without marvelling at the obstacles overcome and the successes gained. The road, for instance, from Albert to Bapaume, through Pozieres, Le Sars, and Warlincourt, passing close by Contalmaison and Martincourt, was contested almost yard by yard, and the same thing may be said of the road that leads along the bank of the Ancre from Albert past the Leipzig Redoubt, near Thiepval and Beaumont Hamel, through Achiet-le-Grand to Bapaume, or the one from Peronne through Le Transloy.

It was in December 1916 that I paid

F

my first visit to the valley of the Somme. The scene was dreary beyond description. Many villages known to us by name as the scenes of desperate fighting were a name only. Hardly a vestige of a house or cottage remained where many had been before the war. Here and there one could see the entrance to a cellar ; the charred stump of a strafed tree ; the remains of a garden ; or a bit of a cemetery. Everything else was churned up into the most appalling mud.

One day I had tea with an Army commander who has done great things since then, and he showed me a series of photographs—the most interesting I have ever seen, which were taken the day before my visit, by our airmen, over the German lines. For seventeen and a half miles back, the enemy, with infinite care and patience, had constructed trenches, 'and,' said the Commander, ' every time we destroy his front line trench he constructs another one in the rear.' 'But,' I cried, ' if this kind of thing goes on, and unless the unexpected happens, the war must surely continue indefinitely.' His only reply was, ' Is it not always the unexpected that happens in war ? ' I was back again in Picardy in the summer of 1917, and the unexpected had happened. The whole of the seventeen and a half miles of trenches were in the hands of the British ! The enemy had retired to the much advertised ' Hindenburg Line,' and leaving nothing to chance, was tirelessly, ceaselessly massing and training his men, getting together huge reserves of munitions, husbanding his resources in every possible way, and preparing, always preparing day and night for his next great move. Meanwhile, Italy's defences had to be strengthened by troops we could ill-afford to spare from our Western front, and Russia, in loyalty to whom we first entered the war, failed us altogether, German intrigue being the underlying cause in each case. In his great advance in March and April 1918 he did not achieve all he set out to do by any means, but his gains were enormous. It makes one sad to think of the territory we had temporarily to relinquish to the Hun in Picardy, even though the country itself was not of any intrinsic value. The land is desolate, and the enemy ruined every village and hamlet, every farm and cottage, before his retreat. Ninety-three Red Triangle centres—huts, marquees, cellars, dug-outs, and ' strafed ' houses had to be abandoned in Picardy alone—most of them destroyed before they fell into the hands of the Germans.

During the first visit to the battlefields of the Somme in the winter of 1916, the outstanding feature of the landscape was the mud and the general desolation. In the summer of 1917 the scenes of desolation were as great as ever, but there was a difference—the roads were in excellent condition and bridges had been replaced. There were shell-holes everywhere and the countryside was strewn with dud shells; barbed wire entanglements; with here and there a stranded tank that had had to be abandoned in the mud; the remains of trenches and dug-outs or the cages in which the Huns had collected their British prisoners. There were no domestic animals to be seen, and no civilians. The whole district from Albert to Peronne, to Bapaume or to Arras, was one huge cemetery, and one saw side by side the elaborate cross that marked the burying place of German dead, the smaller cross with the tricolour on it, that marked the last resting-place of the soldier of France, and everywhere for miles and miles could be seen the little plain brown crosses of wood, that marked the

spot where lay our own loved dead. We
climbed to the top of the famous Butte of
Warlincourt that so often changed hands
in the course of desperate fighting, and
there on the top were those little brown
crosses. We stood at the edge of the vast
crater of La Boiselle that inaugurated the
first battle of the Somme and saw in its
depths several of those little symbols of
our Christian faith, but looking away
across the desolation of the battlefield one
marvelled at the efforts of nature to hide
up the ravages of war. There were the
most glorious masses of colour everywhere—the colour given by the wild
flowers of the battlefields. One felt one
had never seen more vivid blue than that
of the acres of cornflowers which rivalled
the hues of the gentian of the Alps. It
may have been imagination, but looking
out from the Butte of Warlincourt over
miles of poppies, one felt one had never

seen such vivid red, and instinctively those words came into one's mind :

> ' O Cross that liftest up my head,
>   I dare not seek to fly from thee ;
>   I lay in dust life's glory dead,
>   And from the ground there blossoms red,
>   Life that shall endless be.'

The wild flowers of Picardy have bloomed over British graves again in the summer of 1918, though German, not British, eyes saw them during the early months, but those flowers speak of eternal hope, and tell us that if we but do our part, the sacrifice of our bravest and best will not have been made in vain.

Amid the ruins of Picardy the Y.M.C.A did some of its best work. Lord Derby spoke of the Association as 'essential in peace time, indispensable in war time,' and never was the Association more indispensable than during those terrible days of the German advance in 1918. Amid the ever-changing scenes of war it has been one of the forces working for reconstruction. We mourn the loss of huts and Red Triangle centres that have cost money, and on which labour has been lavished. Not much to look at many of these places, and yet to those who knew them they possessed an indescribable charm and fascination. 'It was only a little marquee, for instance, that formed the Headquarters of the Red Triangle at Henin in 1917, only a couple of padres, one Church of England and one a Free Churchman there to represent the Y.M.C.A., but the whole story is a romance. Whilst we were sharing their lunch of bully beef and potatoes, bread, biscuits, and coffee, a 'strafe' began. The British artillery, half a mile away, were pouring lead into the Hun lines. Fritz soon replied, and things became lively. A shell burst near us, but our padres took no notice of it, and seemed to regard a little incident of that kind as a ·matter of course. Another shell burst on the cross-roads we had just traversed. It was here we had our first glimpse of the Hindenburg Line with Crucifix Corner in the foreground. Whilst we were still at lunch the Germans began to throw over some of their heavy stuff in the direction of Monchy, which was not far away. The British camp at Henin had been heavily bombarded a few days before our visit, and the troops quite properly had to run like rabbits to their burrows. The last to take refuge in the dug-outs were our two padres, who with a keen and commendable sense of duty had waited to gather up the cash before taking refuge from the shells. One of the leaders gives the following graphic story of his experiences in the Retreat :—

'On the first day of the offensive we were wakened by terrific drum fire to the north, but on our own immediate stretch of front, the firing was not so severe. There was therefore no immediate need for evacuation. During that day the hut work went on as usual, but few men appeared, as everybody was "standing to." Liquid nourishment of the Y.M.C.A. type was rather at a discount. We finished serving at a somewhat late hour, and deemed it advisable to sleep in the dug-out, as a few shells had begun to sing overhead. Early the next morning we were awakened by the sound of many men on the move. More and still more French troops were arriving, and that day we had to speak more French than English. Towards evening uncomfortable reports began to arrive that the Germans had several places behind us, some in the immediate rear. "Les avions Boche," about which the Frenchmen were using " polite " phrases all day, were continually overhead, and having reported the movement of troops on the roads, shell-fire began to increase in intensity. Decidedly, it was " getting warm." Lieutenant-Colonel —— of the R.A.M.C. and the Medical Staff with whom I had had the privilege of messing for some time were very forcible in their advice to me to evacuate with the orderlies. They were living in a shell - proof dug-out, whereas we had no possible defence against a direct hit from any kind of shell.

'Several batteries of artillery having been withdrawn from forward positions, and posted near us, were making sleep impossible and drawing the enemy's fire. It was quite impossible to obtain transport of any kind for my stores, so I gave what remained to the R.A.M.C. for walking wounded cases, of which I had supplied several during the day.

'Then we made a "night-flitting," the orderlies and myself, and slept a few miles to the S.W. But with every step away from the hut I became more and more uncomfortable. ·By daybreak I had decided to return and see how things were going. The orderlies decided to accompany me.

' On the way back we had to take cover once for a while, but finally reached the hut and carried on for the remainder of the day.

' We were called several kinds of lunatics for returning by the Medical Staff, who were then preparing to leave, and be it confessed we felt the truth of their remarks. It was quite out of the question to hold on any longer without cover save a " tin-hat " a-piece, so again we evacuated, this time finally.'

It was only when the grey-clad Germans were actually in sight that the workers at St. Leger left their loved Y.M.C.A. I only visited St. Leger once, but that little shanty strangely fascinated me. It was not much to look at, just a group of ruined farm buildings, and in it ' the swallows had found a house ' and regardless of our presence, yes, regardless of the shells, for St. Leger was bombarded every day even then, they flew backwards and forwards, feeding their young and twittering merrily and unconcernedly as if it had been a farm building in one of our English counties. It must have been with a heavy heart that those Y.M.C.A. men turned their backs on St. Leger and trudged to Boisleaux-au-Mont, where the five splendid huts that formed our equipment shortly afterwards shared the fate of St. Leger, and were all destroyed before the advance of the Huns.

At Boyelles the tent was amid the ruins by the roadside, and the enamelled Triangle sign was attached to the bottom of the trunk of a tree that had been cut down by the enemy and was lying in the hedge just as it fell. Achiet-le-Petit Y.M.C.A. was in an orchard, the equipment consisting of a big marquee and several little shanties ingeniously constructed by the workers from empty petrol cans and biscuit boxes. High up in an elm tree was a sort of crow's nest, used by the Germans as an observation post during the time of their occupation. At Haplincourt the Y.M.C.A. was anything but imposing—an insignificant house fitted up as a club room, but in the paddock behind it the secretaries had erected a platform, and arranged an open-air auditorium on a grand scale. A hundred yards or so away was a large plunge bath, deep enough for a good high dive. It had been constructed by the Germans when they were in occupation, but when we saw it a score of our own Tommies were disporting themselves in the water and having a high old time. Albert was a scene of desolation, with its ruined church as the most conspicuous feature. High up on the top of the spire, dislodged by German shells, and jutting out at right angles to the spire, was the famous figure of the Virgin holding in her hands the infant Christ. For many months the figure had remained in this position, and was only finally brought down during the enemy's advance in 1918. The Y.M.C.A. in Albert was established in one big hut and two badly ruined houses. It was on the Saturday that St. Leger fell, and the Sunday at Albert was a memorable day. The town was crowded with an endless stream of men, horses, guns, and service wagons passing through. Little was sold in our canteens, but free refreshments were handed out by tired but willing workers all day long. Nearly all those workers had thrilling stories to tell of narrow escapes from death. Albert was evacuated on the Sunday night, and the place must have presented somewhat the appearance of a shambles. The Boche aeroplanes were dropping bombs or firing their machine-guns all the time, but still our men kept on serving the hot tea and cocoa, biscuits, and cigarettes that were so much appreciated by officers and men alike, only leaving their posts and abandoning their hut when ordered to do so by the Military. The retreat from Albert must have been like an awful nightmare. Some of our men in the darkness became entangled in the fallen wires, and whilst trying to extricate themselves heard the hum of an aeroplane just overhead, and a bomb was dropped only a few yards in front of them.

At Bapaume we had several centres in and closely adjacent to the town. Bapaume, like Peronne, was not destroyed by enemy shell-fire, but deliberately wrecked by the Hun before he was forced to evacuate, and the foe we face to-day is

THE Y.M.C.A. IN A RUINED WAREHOUSE. SHELL-HOLE IN FLOOR OF CANTEEN

A Y.M.C.A. CELLAR AT YPRES

a past master in the art of destruction. Hardly a building of any description remained intact in either of these towns when the British entered into occupation. That very fact made us marvel when, standing for the first time in front of the big building occupied by the Y.M.C.A. in Peronne we noticed that it was practically intact. On entering the building we marvelled still more, for the first object we saw was a fine German piano. Surely it was an act of kindness on the part of the wily Hun to leave it for our men. Was it ? When the British occupied Peronne a company of troops from the west of England were the first to enter that house. A Tommy who was musical made a bee-line for the piano, but his officer restrained him, bidding him first look inside. It was well he did so, for three powerful bombs were attached to the strings of the piano, and had he touched one of the keys concerned, he himself, the piano, and the building would have been utterly destroyed. In the hut attached to the house a boxing match was taking place on the evening of our arrival, and men had come from outposts miles away to take part. Underneath the house was a German dug-out of almost incredible depth. The original staircase was missing —the Germans having commandeered the wood for the construction of the dug-out —but it had been replaced by an ingenious Y.M.C.A. secretary, who had searched amid the ruins of Peronne until at last he had found another staircase, which, with infinite pains and labour and not a little ingenuity, he had built in to replace the original one. The day before our visit the old lady who had lived in the house before the war paid a visit to her old home. She was a refugee, and had trudged miles to get back to Peronne. She requested permission to dig in the garden and soon unearthed the uniform of her husband who fought against the Germans in 1870. She had buried it there before the fall of the town. Digging again she came across his sword and accoutrements, and deeper still, her silver spoons and other trinkets that she valued. Could anything bring home more clearly the horrors of war? If, instead of Peronne in Northern France, it had been that sweet little town in England or Scotland, or that village in Wales or Ireland in which you live! If you had heard the cry one evening, 'The Huns are coming,' and had just half an hour in which to rush round your home and gather together any things you specially treasured, — and take them out into your garden and bury them, knowing that anything you left behind would be either looted and sent to Germany, or deliberately destroyed for sheer hate! How easily this

might have been, but for the mercy of
God, the mistakes and miscalculations of
the enemy, and the bravery and self-
sacrifice of our heroes in blue and khaki,
yes, and our workers in fustian and print
—for England must never forget the debt
she owes to her munition workers as well
as to her sailors, soldiers, and airmen.
They see nothing of the romance of war ;
they know nothing of its excitement, and
yet apart from their patriotic service the
best efforts of our fighting men would have
been in vain.

Never was the Y.M.C.A. more appreciated than during the months that pre-
ceded the great retreat in the spring of
1918. New Red Triangle huts were spring-
ing up like mushrooms, especially in the
Fifth Army area, that part of the line that
had recently been taken over from the
French. Supported by the generous gifts
of friends at home, ably directed by our

.divisional secretaries and those associated with them in the work, and supported and encouraged in every way by the Military Authorities, the progress made was remarkable. Then came the unexpected advance of the German hordes and the laborious work of months was destroyed in a few hours. At Noyon the secretary had to quit in a hurry, but returned to the hut later to bring away the money belonging to the Y.M.C.A. Thrice he returned, and the third time found it impossible to get away. After remaining in hiding for twenty-four hours he at length managed to escape with ten thousand francs in his pocket, saved for the Association which lost so heavily during those terrible days. At Amiens the Y.M.C.A. workers hung on for ten days after the official canteens had been removed because the town had become too hot for them. Day and night the ' Joy ' hut close to the railway station was kept open, and thronged with officers and men, and the service rendered to the troops may be gauged from the amount of the takings, which ranged between fifteen and twenty thousand francs a day.

Our total loss in the retreat was exceedingly heavy—more than one hundred and thirty huts and other centres in Picardy and Flanders, and in cash, upwards of one hundred and fifty thousand pounds. Serious as was that loss it might have been very much worse. Eight trucks of stores and equipment were stopped in the nick of time. The axle of one of our big lorries broke within a hundred yards of the most heavily shelled area in one of the towns bombarded by the enemy, but it was got away and, excepting in two cases, all the money and notes from tills and cash-boxes were removed safely before the huts were abandoned—striking testimony to the devotion of those in charge.

' What I think impressed me most,' wrote the organising secretary for France, ' has been the undaunted spirit of our workers, who, when shelled out of huts, persisted in the attempt to return to them under very great personal danger.' ' Although we have lost everything that we had,' wrote one, ' we still have hope within us, and are trusting to get back right into the thick of things in the very near future.' Yet another, writing in the spirit of Eastertide, said, ' We believe that our work will rise in new freshness and power out of its apparent extinction ! ' ' There was a singular unanimity of effort on the part of the workers who were isolated one from the other, and had no opportunity of arranging a common policy. The sale of such articles as the soldiers needed continued in the huts up to the last moment possible, and then, when the danger of the hut and stores falling into

the hands of the enemy became imminent,
biscuits and cigarettes were handed out as
largely as possible to men in the neighbourhood taking part in the fighting.
One would have thought that having done
this the workers would have considered
their own personal safety and retired,
but in several cases I found them running
stunts for walking wounded in the open,
outside the hut or in its immediate
neighbourhood, in close touch with the
medical authorities.

'The confusion of the retreat opened up
to our workers opportunities of service
which they gladly utilised. Last night
was a night of uncertainty. We could
not go to bed owing to the uncertainty
of the military position where our headquarters were, and so stood on a high hill
beside an old Trappist monastery, watching
the village at the foot in flames, and trying
to ascertain the progress of the fighting

through the darkness. Our workers even under these circumstances seized an opportunity of doing a very fine bit of service. A stream of poor refugees were passing, people of all conditions and ages, fleeing for safety and shelter, and so at 11.30 at night at the cross-roads, a table was set up with a hot urn of cocoa and supplies of biscuits, which were handed out to French and Flemish people as they passed. . . .

'I have never seen anything that has touched me more than these streams of all sorts and conditions of people straggling along with their little belongings, infants in arms, to old people who had not walked a mile for years. It was a great opportunity for rendering a truly Christian service. The other day we lent one of our large lorries for a whole day for the purpose of carrying these people in some degree of comfort to a place of safety.'

Thus by every device that resourcefulness and experience could suggest the workers of the Y.M.C.A. in France minis-tered to the comfort of the men who were so bravely sustaining that terrible on-slaught. The organisation of the Red Triangle is the embodied goodwill of the British people towards its beloved army. An emergency like the one in the spring of 1918 was just the time when the services of the Red Triangle were most sorely needed by our soldiers.

Fortunately, all the Y.M.C.A. workers got away safely. Sixty from the Fifth Army took refuge at Amiens, whilst more than eighty from the area of the Third Army found sanctuary at Doullens.

A few months later, thanks to the arrival of the Americans in France, and the brilliant strategy of Foch and Haig; thanks above all to the mercy of God, the tide turned, and the Huns were once more in full retreat. A distinguished war cor-

respondent wrote his impressions of
Bapaume a day or two after it had again
been captured by the British. Said he,
'I prowled about the streets of Bapaume
through gaping walls of houses, over
piled wreckage, and found it the same old
Bapaume as when I had left it, except that
some of our huts and an officers' club, and
some Y.M.C.A. tents and shelters have
been blown to bits like everything else.'
A ruined town without a Y.M.C.A.!
Could anything be more desolate?

CHAPTER VIII

THE BARRAGE AND AFTER

The problem of dealing with conditions, at such a time, and under existing circumstances, at the rest camps has always been a most difficult one; but the erection of huts by the Young Men's Christian Association has made this far easier.

The extra comfort thereby afforded to the men, and the opportunities for reading and writing, have been of incalculable service, and I wish to tender to your Association, and all those who have assisted, my most grateful thanks.—FIELD-MARSHAL VISCOUNT FRENCH.

IT was on the afternoon of July 30, 1917, that we reached Bailleul in Flanders. Proceeding directly to the Headquarters of the Y.M.C.A. we had tea, and then set out to visit the huts in the vicinity. It was a novel experience, for every hut was empty. The reason was not far to find. The troops were in their camps formed up in marching order, and later in the evening we watched them march out to take part in the great offensive. We were told that the barrage was timed for 3.50 in the morning, and were asked to have our work for the walking wounded ready at 5 A.M., so we determined to spend the night on the top of Kemmel Hill, the highest hill in Flanders. It was just after midnight when we reached the summit of the hill; and we wondered if the barrage had not already commenced, so heavy was the firing. From our point of vantage we could see the whole of the sector, from Armentières in the south, across the battlefields of Messines and Wytschaete and away beyond Ypres in the north. Silently, close to us, an observation balloon stole up in the darkness, and a few minutes later as silently descended. Involuntarily we ducked as a monster shell shrieked overhead, and some one cried, 'There goes the Bailleul Express!' About 3 A.M. things began to quiet down. Our guns might have been knocked out ; they were hardly replying at all to the enemy's fire. Later on we saw a series of signal flashes high up across the battlefield, and then at 3.50 promptly to the moment, the barrage began, and there was no possibility of mistaking it—two thousand guns, as we learned afterwards, all firing at the same time. As one looked at that hell of flame and bursting shell, one felt it was impossible for any life to continue to exist beneath it, and one thought of the boys, as steady as if they had been on parade, creeping up behind that barrage of fire. We had seen them as they left their camp the night before, and we saw them when they returned—some of them—during the two days following the barrage ; not in regiments a thousand strong, with colours flying and bands playing, but dribbling back one or two at a time—the walking wounded—and each one came in to our little Y.M.C.A. tents attached to the clearing stations—one was at an island in a sea of mud, near Dickebusch huts in Flanders. There was a queue inside of two or three hundred men. Every man in that queue was wounded, and waiting to have his wounds attended to ; every man was hungry until he entered that tent ; every man plastered from head to foot with the most appalling mud, and unless one has seen the mud of Flanders or of the Somme, it is impossible to imagine what it is really like. As I mingled with the men in that queue and assisted our workers to hand out hot tea, coffee, and cocoa, biscuits, bread and butter, chocolate, cigarettes or oranges, I thanked God for the opportunity He had given to the Y.M.C.A., and the thing that impressed me more than anything else was the fact that one did not hear a single complaint, not one word of grousing. And why not ? Was it because they liked that kind of thing ? Don't make any mistake about it—no one could possibly like it, but out there the men know they are fighting not for truth and freedom in the abstract, but for their own liberty, and, what is infinitely more important to them, for their homes and loved ones. They know that what the Hun has done for Northern France and Flanders is as nothing compared with what he would do for the places and the people we love if he once got the opportunity of wreaking his vengeance on us. There is no finer bit of work that the Y.M.C.A. is doing to-day than this work for the walking wounded, which before any great push takes place, is carefully organised down to the last detail. Before one of the great battles, our men took up their positions at thirty-four different centres where they were able to minister to the

HUT IN WILDERNESS OF DESTRUCTION.   CUTTING THE ICE IN SHELL-HOLES
FOR WATER FOR TEA—WINTER, 1916-17

RUINED HOUSE USED BY Y.M.C.A., PROPPED UP BY TIMBER

needs of the wounded, and thus to co-
operate with the magnificent work that is
being done under the sign of the Red Cross.
As in France, so in Italy and in the East,
at Beersheba and other centres on the lines
of communication in Palestine, records show
how efficiently the same type of service is
being rendered to our brave troops.

To return to the barrage. It is always
interesting to note the effect a scene of
that kind has on people of different
temperaments. We had been sitting round
a huge shell-hole near the top of Kemmel
Hill feeling, it must be confessed, a trifle
'fed-up' with things. We were all tired,
and had had a very heavy day's work.
It was an uncomfortable night, to say the
least of it, with drizzling rain, and very
cold for the time of year. At the first
sound of the drum-fire of the barrage
set up by the British guns, we sprang to our
feet, wild with excitement. A distinguished

H

padre from the Midlands was lost in admiration for the work of the munitioners whose labours made possible this great strafing of the Hun. The leader of the party, a colonial from far-off Australia, simply danced with excitement which he made no attempt to suppress, contenting himself with ejaculating from time to time expressions to the effect that that was the most dramatic moment of his life. An unemotional Professor from one of our great universities stood with clenched fists, and was overheard to say, ' Give 'em hell, boys ! ' Another padre in the company began to quote Browning, the quotation referring to the signal flashes to which reference has already been made :

> ' From sky to sky. Sudden there went,
>   Like horror and astonishment,
>   A fierce vindictive scribble of red,
>   Which came across, as if one said,
>   . . . " There—
>   " Burn it ! " '

How often it happens that in the greatest moments of one's life, it is the trivial thing that appeals most strongly to one's imagination. So in this case. The thing never to be forgotten was connected with the early dawn. I can see even now that long grey streak on the horizon across the battlefield, as the daylight came. A thrush from a bush close to where we were standing began to pour out its song of praise and thanksgiving, heedless of falling shells and the roar of guns. There was something unspeakably pathetic in that song on the battlefield, yes, and prophetic of the great day that is coming in spite of all reverses; the day of victory and peace, peace purchased at the price of struggle, and of blood.

As one watched the barrage from Kemmel the onslaught seemed to be irresistible. It seemed impossible for the German hordes to hold our men back. Neither could they have held them, but what the Hun could not do, the rain did for him. It just teemed down, and in a few hours Flanders was churned up into a swamp of mud. It was impossible to bring the big guns up and the whole advance was stayed. One thought how often the same thing had happened before, and wondered, only wondered, if we at home were supporting the boys at the Front as they had a right to expect us to support them? It is so easy at a time like this to put one's trust merely in 'reeking tube and iron shard,' and to leave God out of our calculations. After all in this great struggle we are not fighting merely against 'flesh and blood,' but against 'principalities and powers, against spiritual wickedness in high places,' and even to-day 'More things are wrought by prayer than this world dreams of.' It was that great soldier, Sir William Robertson, who said, "Let us never forget in all that we do that the measure of our ultimate success will be governed largely, if not mainly, by the extent to which we put our religious convictions into our actions, and hold fast, firmly and fearlessly, to the faith of our forefathers.' Had the Germans beaten us two years ago every one would have known the reason why —they had more men, bigger guns, and more of them, more aeroplanes, and an infinitely better supply of munitions of war, but by the summer of 1917 we were superior to them in every particular, and yet victory tarried. Why? Can it be that God was waiting for His people to seek His aid?

With Russia out of the war, we were once again to stand with our backs to the wall—the position in which the British are always seen at their best—and the National crisis came as one more challenge to the Nation to turn to the God of our fathers.

CHAPTER IX

'LES PARENTS BLESSÉES'

The Y.M.C.A.? Why, they could no more do without the Y.M.C.A. than they could do without munitions at the Front? I have seen it in operation.—THE RIGHT HON. WILL CROOKS, M.P.

'A GREAT Mother Hen,' so wrote one who for the first time saw the work of the Y.M.C.A. for the relatives of dangerously wounded men. This work is carried on in London and a number of provincial centres, but it is seen at its best in France, for there it is on a much larger scale. If a man is dangerously wounded and lying in one of the hospitals on the other side of the Channel, a message is sent to his people at home containing the requisite permission to visit him, and telling them, moreover, that from the moment they

reach France the Y.M.C.A. will take care
of them. Red Triangle motors meet every
boat as it reaches a French port ; auto-
matically the relatives of wounded, or
' Les Parents Blessées ' as the French call
them, are handed over to our care, and
we motor them to their destination—
assisted sometimes by the Red Cross. As
this may mean a run of eighty or a hundred
miles, and in war time may mean a whole
day, or possibly two days on the French
railways, the motor run is in itself a great
boon. During the whole of the time they
are in France, the relatives are entertained
as the guests of the Red Triangle in the
special hostels that have been established
for the purpose in the principal bases.
Many of them have never been away from
their own homes before ; they know no
language but their own, and a journey
of the kind would have its terrors at any
time, but to all the ordinary difficulties

has now to be added the fact that they are consumed with anxiety on account of those who are dearer than life itself. It means everything to them that the Y.M.C.A. as a 'Great Mother Hen' takes them under its protection, soothes and protects them, so that in the darkest moments of their lives they are not dealt with by any officials who have to get through so many cases in a given time, but by sympathetic friends, actuated only by the love of God, and of country. One of the most beautiful of these hostels is 'Les Iris.' It is hidden away in the depths of a wood near the sea, and in the springtime the nights are full of the melody of the nightingales. This hostel is reserved largely for the use of the relatives of dangerously wounded officers. The lady who presides over another of the hostels has been called the Florence Nightingale of the Red Triangle, and indeed that would be a suitable name for any of these ladies who take the relatives to their hearts, and do everything possible to comfort and cheer them and make them feel at home. As we write, a letter from one of our guests lies before us. We quote from it because it is typical of thousands of letters received from grateful friends :—

'Many thanks for the photo of my son's grave received this morning. How very kind you Y.M.C.A. people are. I little thought last November when I was begging (Hut Week in Brighton) that I should reap personal benefit from the Y.M.C.A. The kindness and hospitality extended to my husband and I when we came to France nearly three months ago, we shall never forget. It is not in our power to help with money except in a small way, but we tell all we can, and help in every way in our power.'

During a recent visit to France we had the privilege of being shown over one of the British hospitals, which, like all our hospitals, was wonderfully efficient. Everything that could be done to alleviate suffering was done. In one ward every man was seriously wounded, and side by side were two beds, one occupied by a young Canadian and the other by a young Britisher. The latter had his mother with him, who was one of our guests. The Canadian watched them together for some time in silence, but followed them with his eyes as a cat might a mouse. Suddenly, without any warning, he flung himself over on to his side and burst out crying. Questioned as to what was the matter, he replied, 'Nothing.' 'Then what makes you cry? Is the pain worse?' 'No, thanks, the pain is better.' 'Then what makes you cry like that?' Drying his eyes, the boy replied, 'It's all very well for him, he's got his mother with him. My mother is more than six thousand miles away!' Is it not worth any effort and any cost to help the loved ones of these men who have made such great sacrifices for us? The whole of this work for ' Les Parents Blessées ' is full of pathos. On one occasion we reached a big hospital centre just as another Association car arrived from a big base port, bringing three English women to see their husbands. The Y.M.C.A. leader took them to the wards they were seeking. At the first, the sister in charge came to speak to one of our guests and said, ' I am very sorry, but am afraid your husband won't know you. He has been terribly ill, and all sorts of complications have set in, but you had better come in and see him.' Twenty minutes later we saw her again, and she told us that for ten minutes she sat by her husband's bedside, but he did not know her. Then stooping over him, she whispered, 'You remember little Lizzie and little Willie at home, don't you?' For one second he gave her that look of love and recognition that made the long journey from home worth while.

Passing on to another ward we sent in a message, and the sister came to greet our guest, and said, 'I am glad to say your husband is much better. I'll tell him you are here.' When she same back she said she had asked the invalid, 'What would you like best in all the world?' Without a moment's hesitation, he replied, 'To go back to Blighty, Sister.' 'Blighty'— how many of those who use it realise the meaning of the word? It comes from the Indian 'Vilayhti' and means 'The home across the sea.' 'Blighty!' said the Sister; 'you know that's impossible. What would you like next best?' 'To see my wife,' was the prompt reply. 'And what would you say if I told you your wife was waiting outside to see you ? ' queried the Sister, as she moved from his bedside and opened the door. Yes, to these people many thousands of them, the Red Triangle has indeed been as a Great Mother Hen at a time when they most needed its care. We are all very much like big children, and to all of us there are times when we need some one to take us by the hand and speak words of consolation and good cheer.

CHAPTER X

CELLARS AND DUG-OUTS ON THE WESTERN FRONT

My son, who is somewhere in France, tells me what a great comfort your Y.M.C.A. has been to him from the time he started his training at —— and all through his stopping-places almost up to the trenches.

UNLESS one has seen for oneself the ravages of war, it is impossible to conceive the horror and desolation of a place like Ypres. Before the war it was one of the most beautiful cities in Europe, to-day it is nothing more than a heap of ruins. It is enough to make even the most unemotional of men cry, to stand in that once beautiful Cloth Hall Square and see how complete is the destruction—not one house, not a single room left intact—everything destroyed beyond recognition. And

what of the Y.M.C.A. in Ypres ?   There
we found the Red Triangle standing erect
amid the ruins, and following the hand
that pointed down we came to a little
cellar Y.M.C.A.—only a cellar and yet it
had been a source of helpfulness and
inspiration to tens of thousands of our
brave men.   It was wonderfully fitted up,
contained a small circulating library, piano,
and everything needed for the canteen
side of things.   Not only that, it was a
centre to work from.   Between the cellar
and the enemy were nine dug-outs at
advanced stations.   As these were all
evacuated by order of the Military during
the German offensive in April 1918, there
can be no objection to their location being
indicated.   The first consisted of a ruined
house and a Nissen hut at the Asylum ;
the second was at ' Salvation Corner,' and
the third at Dead End, on the Canal bank.
There was a Y.M.C.A. at Wells Cross

Roads, another at St. Jean and Wiel, and a sixth at Potyze Château. The seventh had a homely ring about it, for it was situated at 'Oxford Circus,' the eighth was at St. Julien, the ninth at Lille Gate (Ypres), and the tenth was the cellar Y.M.C.A. at the corner of Lille Road referred to above. For many months it was the centre of the social life of the stricken town, but in August 1917 it received a direct hit from an enemy shell, and was knocked in. This dug-out work is intensely interesting, though naturally it has its limitations. Large meetings are, of course, impossible ; sometimes even the singing of a hymn would be sufficient to attract the attention of Fritz, but the man who is resourceful and courageous, and who can see an opportunity for Christian service in meeting the common everyday needs of men, will find endless opportunities of putting in a word for the Master—and

CANADIAN Y.M.C.A. DUG-OUT IN A MINE CRATER ON VIMY RIDGE, 1917

A CANADIAN Y.M.C.A. DUG-OUT NEAR VIMY RIDGE

the sordid dug-out under shell-fire, can
easily be transformed into a temple to
His praise, an inquiry-room where resolu-
tions are made that change the lives of
men, and help the soldier to realise that he
is called to be a crusader.

In the Red Triangle dug-outs of the
Ypres salient, from three to four thousand bloaters were supplied to the troops
week by week; 1500 kilos of apples, and
more than 100,000 eggs ! It was a miracle
how these latter were collected in the
villages behind the line. Corps provided
a lorry and two drivers for five months to
bring them into Ypres, and also assisted
us with thirty orderlies. It was that
timely help that made our work possible.
It would be difficult to overestimate the
boon to the troops of this variety to their
diet. Iron rations will keep body and
soul together, but it is the little extra
that helps so much in keeping up the

I

health and spirits of the men. They would follow the egg lorry for a mile and gladly pay the threepence each that the eggs cost. In February 1918, the turnover from the Red Triangle centres round Ypres amounted to 245,000 francs, whilst in March it had risen to 260,000. For many weeks in this salient we gave away from five to six thousand gallons of hot drinks each week. All honour to the band of Y.M.C.A. leaders who kept the Red Triangle flag flying under these difficult conditions. For six weeks one of our leaders was unable to leave his cellar home, owing to the incessant shelling and bombing of the immediate vicinity. These were men who 'counted not their own lives dear unto them,' but were ready to take any risk and to put up with any personal inconvenience that they might serve the country they loved—yes, and they too endured 'as seeing Him Who is invisible.'

The King, who is the patron of the

Y.M.C.A., and very keenly interested in the work, visited our tiny centre at Messines. The dug-out at Wytschaete was knocked out, and the Red Triangle cellar at Meroc, just behind Loos, destroyed by a direct hit. The latter was approached by a long communication trench, and was fitted up in the ordinary way—a few tables and chairs, reading and writing materials, games, pictures on the walls, and, of course, the inevitable and always appreciated piano. A few days before we were there a dud shell from one of the German 'heavies' fell only two or three yards in front of the divisional secretary's car. The cellar was immediately under a ruined *brasserie*, and in the grounds of the latter was a solitary German grave. The story goes that in the early days of the war enemy patrols passed through Meroc, and a shot alleged to have been fired from a window of the *brasserie* found its billet in one of the

Huns. In revenge, the Germans killed every man, woman, and child in the *brasserie*. In striking contrast was the story told us by the matron of one of our British hospitals : ' Every one in this ward is desperately wounded, and too ill to travel. All in that row,' said she, pointing, ' are Germans. Yesterday a man occupying one of those beds lay dying, and could not make his head comfortable. I went into the next ward, and said to the Tommies " There's a German dying, will one of you lend him your pillow ? " Without a moment's hesitation,' said she, ' every one of those dangerously wounded Britishers whipped out his pillow to help his dying enemy.' That is the spirit of our men, and that accounts, quite as much as their valour, for the fact that they have won the respect even of an enemy trained from infancy to regard the British soldier as an object of scorn and derision.

CHAPTER XI

CAMEOS FROM FRANCE

The work of this Young Men's Christian Association has sunk so deep into the minds and into the lives of our fellow countrymen that its work in the future can never be diminished, and must be extended. And it is going to do more to my mind, than simply minister to the wants of the men in camp ; it is going to be a bond between this country and the Great Englands beyond the sea.—THE RT. HON. THE EARL OF DERBY, K.G., G.C.V.O.

A STRIKING feature of the war work of the Y.M.C.A. has been the promptness with which a new situation has been seized and a new opening entered. There has been an utter absence of red tape, and freedom of action has been given to all accredited representatives of the Association. The Red Triangle has always been first in the field, and has been likened to a tank in its knack of overcoming apparently insuperable obstacles. The day after the British troops first entered Bapaume a Y.M.C.A. man appeared leading a packhorse loaded up with cigarettes, biscuits, and dolly cakes, which he distributed amongst the troops. He had got a foothold for the Association, and that foothold was retained until Bapaume was evacuated.

*　　*　　*

In the British offensive in the early days of August 1918 a noted war correspondent at the Front wrote :— -

'In one part of the line three hours after the troops reached their final objective they were eating a hot breakfast as part of the programme of the day. The familiar, ever-welcome sign of the " Y.M.C.A." blossomed on a roofless French café six miles within the crumpled German line, before the tanks had finished chasing the 11th Corps staff out of Framerville and down the Peronne road. Food, and even books and papers, were set out under the Red Triangle for tired and hungry fighting men as they trooped into the rickety building to eat and be refreshed in a room carpeted with German papers.'

* * *

What thrilling memories the name of Arras will always conjure up in the minds of Y.M.C.A. workers who served in that city of ruins! One wrote home the day after a strong attack by the British on the enemy lines. He wrote the letter from a dug-out which only the day before was occupied by the Huns, in which he was carrying on for the Y.M.C.A. So precipitate was their flight that he partook of the repast served up by German cooks for German officers. At one time the rival trenches were, in places, less than ten yards apart! It was here that Sir Douglas Haig personally complimented the Association on the work its representatives were doing on the field of battle.

The most memorable motor run we ever had was from Souastre to Arras in 1916. The hut was closed when we reached Souastre in the morning, the leader having received a letter from the Town Major politely requesting him to close it from 7.30 A.M. as it was expected that the Huns would strafe the village at 8 A.M., and again at 4.30, and so it happened. This seemed strange, as the village had not been strafed of late. How could the British have known when Fritz would fire again ? It seemed uncanny, until a strange unwritten reciprocal working arrangement between friend and foe was explained, which means in effect that Fritz refrains from bombing or bombarding ' A——' three or four miles behind the British lines if Tommy leaves village ' B——' behind his lines alone, and *vice versa*. As both villages are used as billets for the rival armies, both have been glad at times to honour this understanding. The run from Souastre to the railhead at Saulty was uneventful.   Night was closing in as we left for Arras and there was no moon.   For twenty kilos or more we had to travel with lights extinguished.   We were less than a mile from the enemy trenches, which ran parallel to the road we were traversing.   'Verey' lights or star-shells sent up by the enemy continually made everything as light as day for the few seconds they were in the air.   There were mysterious noises from the gun emplacements that run along the roadside, and mysterious shapes loomed up ahead of us from time to time as we overhauled and passed transport wagons and the like. At last we reached our destination, and it was the writer's first visit to a town of considerable size that had been wrecked by bombardment.   There were barricades

in the streets, shell-holes and ruins everywhere. We motored through the famous
Grande Place and passed through street
after street in that city of the dead, until,
turning a corner, we entered a narrow street
near the ruined cathedral, and hearing a
piano playing rag-time, it was obvious
that we were near the Y.M.C.A. The
memory of that old château in the narrow
street will always remain with us as we
saw it then—the entrance hall, where free
hot drinks were being dispensed; the
canteen crammed with British soldiers,
including many ' Bantams,' who were then
stationed at Arras ; the little concert-room,
with possibly a hundred men gathered
round a piano singing choruses and snatches
of songs or listening to the rag-time,
accompanying it at times by whistling the
refrain or stamping on the floor. Another
crowd upstairs had been entertained to a
lantern lecture, and the day's programme

was being concluded with family prayers.
As we lay awake that night we heard many
familiar noises that sounded strange there
—a cat call, the cry of a baby, whilst ever
and anon a shell would go shrieking over
the town. In the morning we visited the
ruined cathedral, which was a sight to
make men or angels weep, but even there
one saw erect amid the ruins, at the
highest point, the Cross, the emblem of our
Christian faith, and one knew that though
it might be by way of the Cross, yet truth
and freedom would triumph in the end.

*   *   *

A well-known war correspondent writing
from British Headquarters in France to
the *Daily Mail*, on August 13, 1918, told
the story of a village under shell-fire and
still within reach of machine-gun bullets,
in which was a German notice-board
pointing to an incinerator, and wrote :—
' I hear from an officer who visited the

spot again a day later that another notice, "This way to the Y.M.C.A." was added. A dashing cavalry officer, very much of the old school, possessing a voice that would carry two miles, begged me with great earnestness to do him one service, "Would I mention the Y.M.C.A.? It had provided his men with hot coffee before riding out." ' That is the kind of service the Red Triangle has the privilege of rendering to our fighting men in the course of practically every battle.

*   *   *

The Bois Carré in 1916 was a very unhealthy spot. At the edge of a wood in a tiny natural amphitheatre the Y.M.C.A. had one of its outposts. An orderly was usually in charge, and day and night he kept up a good supply of hot drinks for free distribution to the troops. There they could buy biscuits, cigarettes, soap, and other necessaries, or receive free of charge the ever-welcome writing-paper and materials. The supervising secretary visiting the dug-out one day in the course of his rounds found it had been blown in by a big shell. The orderly was terribly wounded, part of his side having been blown away, but smiling amid his agony, he said, ' The money 's safe here, sir ! ' Careless of himself, the brave fellow's first consideration was to safeguard the money in the Y.M.C.A. till.

We have vivid recollections of our visit to the Bois Carré in 1916. Late in the evening we reached Dickebusch. The Y.M.C.A. was there in the main street of the little Belgian village, and immediately behind it was the ruined church. It was only a small strafed building in a ruined street when the Red Triangle first made its appearance in Dickebusch, but the secretary held that to be the most convenient type of Y.M.C.A. building, ' for,' said he, 'if it becomes too small, all you have to do is to knock a hole through the wall on either side, and take in additional houses.' This was exactly what we had done and, unattractive as it was, the place drew crowds of men. At the Dickebusch Y.M.C.A. we were provided with shrapnel and gas helmets and instructed in the use of the latter. A two-mile trudge across a duck-walk over 'b——y meadow' brought us to the famous Ridgewood Dug-outs. It was here that the Canadians lost their guns in the early days of the war, and afterwards so gloriously regained them. We entered the wood at midnight. A huge rat crossed our path, and as we entered the first of the Y.M.C.A. dug-outs where free cocoa was being dispensed in empty jam tins, we remembered a yarn told us the day before by one of our workers. He had come to Ridgewood as a special speaker, and after the evening

meeting lay down on the floor of the dug-
out to sleep, but as he was beginning to
feel drowsy, a huge rat ran over his legs,
and later one passed across his face. With
an electric flash-lamp he scared them
away, but soon getting used to it they came
on ' in close formation.' He lit a candle,
and a few minutes later the rat ran away
with the candle—so he said! From the
Ridgewood we went on to the Bois Carré.
Shells were screaming overhead all the
time, but it was not a long walk though it
provided many thrills. For a couple of
hundred yards we were on open ground,
and within easy reach of the Hun snipers.
Only two of us were allowed to pass at a
time, and my guide and I had to keep
fifty yards apart, and when a ' Verey '
light went up, had to stand absolutely
still until it fell to earth, and its light was
extinguished. Weird things those star
shells! They shoot up to a good height

like rockets, burst into brilliant light,
poise in mid-air and gradually shimmer
down and out. A few minutes brought us
to the shelter of a ruined *brasserie*, and
from its further side we entered the
communication trenches, and thus passed
to the Bois Carré. Standing back to
visualise the scene, the orderly caught my
arm and pulled me into the shelter of the
dug-out—a second later came the patter
of machine bullets on the sand-bags where
we had stood not ten seconds before.
There was something fascinating about
that little dug-out Y.M.C.A., with its
caterer's boiler, urns and stores, and it is
sad to think that since then it has been
destroyed by shell-fire, even though other
dug-outs have been opened to take its
place.

A year later we revisited that old
brasserie. There was little of it left.
The central hall remained, and the Red

A GREAT BOON TO BRITISH TOMMY—A Y.M.C.A.
WELL UNDER SHELL-FIRE

THE CAMBRIDGE DUG-OUT

A REFUGE FOR THE WALKING WOUNDED

Triangle was on it, marking it out as a centre for walking wounded. A dressing station had been rigged up in the cellar underneath. A distinguished preacher serving with the Y.M.C.A. conducted a memorable Watch-night service in the Ridgewood. Two or three hundred men gathered round and listened with marked attention. A shell burst quite close during the prayer, and every man instinctively glanced up to see the effect on the padre. He carried on exactly as if nothing had happened, and won his way to every heart.

K

CHAPTER XII

STORIES OF 'LE TRIANGLE ROUGE'

It is with very great pleasure I send a small
contribution (3s.) to the Y.M.C.A. funds, and only
wish it could match my inclination. Few things
have brought so much comfort to the parents at
home as the knowledge of the splendid work done
by your organisation. As one boy puts it, 'When
we get inside the Y.M.C.A. hut, we feel as if we are
home again.'

AT the close of a Y.M.C.A. Conference held
in the Hôtel McMahon in Paris, a French
lady came timidly forward with a lovely
bouquet of red roses, and in a pretty little
speech presented them as a thankoffering
for the war work of the Y.M.C.A. It was
the gift of a mother who had four sons
serving with the Army. Those flowers
have long since faded, but the kind thought
that prompted them will always remain a
gracious memory.

*   *   *

A soldier home on leave brought an interesting souvenir of the first 'Threapwood' hut, which did such good work in the Ploegsteert Woods, but was ultimately destroyed by shell-fire—a 2 franc and a 50 centimes piece which had become welded together in the heat of the conflagration. Another Tommy saw a fierce fight take place between British and Germans, actually inside the hut at Neuve Église. The incident that seemed to have appealed most strongly to his imagination was the fact that the pictures were still hanging on the walls. It is interesting to notice the curious freaks of dud shells. Outside the hut at Tilloy we saw one which had pierced its way through the trunk of a tree without exploding—the nose of the shell protruded at the other side of the trunk, the shell itself remaining firmly embedded in the tree.

*   *   *

An Australian officer one day sauntered into the 'Crystal Palace,' an important Y.M.C.A. centre in Havre. He was interested, and well he might be. It is a huge building, and swarms of men assemble there in the evenings. The Australian's interest took a practical form. Before leaving he handed two one-pound notes to the leader, expressing regret that he could not make it more, and adding, ' I think you Y.M.C.A. people will make a religious man of me before the war is over.' ' What do you mean ? ' said the secretary. ' Well,' said he, ' I have never had any use for religion, but at the battle of —— I felt down and out. I didn't care much if the Boche killed me. I had had nothing to eat for days— when suddenly a Y.M.C.A. man appeared, heaven knows where he came from, but he was there right enough, and he handed me a good hot drink, a packet of biscuits, and some cigarettes. Yes,' said he, ' I

believe you Y.M.C.A. men will make a
religious man of me before you have
finished.’ -

* * *

In war-time people often forget their
differences, and in Paris one of our splendid
British soldiers, who was a Roman Catholic,
lay badly wounded and terribly ill. He
wanted to confess, but there was no English
priest near. Ultimately a French priest
confessed and absolved him through an
American Y.M.C.A. lady—a Protestant—
who acted as interpreter.

* * *

In the early days of the war a valued
worker on Salisbury Plain was the grandson
of a famous Cornish revivalist. He was
an ordained man and a very strong
Protestant. He went out to France later
on as a chaplain of the United Board.
Returning home on furlough, he called at
Headquarters and told his experiences on

the battlefield. ' You will be surprised,'
said he, ' when I tell you that my greatest
friend in Flanders was a Roman Catholic
padre. He was one of the best men I ever
knew, and we had an excellent working
arrangement. On the battlefield if I came
across any of his men, I would hand them
on to him, and he would pass my men on
to me. If he were not at hand, I would try
my best to help the dying Roman Catholic
soldier as I thought my friend would have
helped him had he been there, and *vice
versa.* I shall never forget,' said he, ' my
last night in Flanders and our affectionate
farewell. You know how strong a
Protestant I have always been, and my
convictions have never been stronger than
they are to-day, but see this,'—and he
unbuttoned his tunic and brought out a
Crucifix which was hanging from his neck
—' this was the parting gift of my Roman
Catholic friend, and as long as I live I shall

keep it as one of my most treasured
possessions.'

*   *   *

As a rule there is not much romance in
the story of a department that concerns
itself with nothing but trading. But the
story of the growth and development of
the trading department of the Red Triangle
is a romance. All along we have discour-
aged trading for trading's sake in our huts,
but in a crisis like the one brought about
by the war, it is not for each individual
or organisation to pick and choose, but to
do what is needed by the State, and on that
principle we have had to develop the
trading side of our work enormously.
Home and overseas, the department has
been brilliantly led by men animated with
the highest ideals of Christian service,
who have been ready to take any risks, and
whenever necessary to work day and
night. Their task has been colossal and

they have done magnificently. During
the six months ending 31st May 1915, our
turnover in France amounted to £32,594,
whilst three years later the six months
turnover had risen to £680,000. It was
thrilling work during the German advance
in March 1918, chasing our ever-moving
centres in the Somme area, and keeping
up their supplies or maintaining touch with
Amiens during these terrible days, when
for a whole week more than £600 daily was
taken in the little ' Joy ' hut outside the
Central Station. That meant day and
night work at our Base Stores in France,
and thanks to the cordial co-operation of the
A.M.F.O. and the H.Q.L. of C. we were
able to send forward 200 trucks from one
port alone, containing 45,000 cases, or 1,500
tons of food-stuffs, smokes, and ingredients
for hot drinks—tea, coffee, and cocoa.
From December 1914 to the middle of
May 1918—1,350,000 cases were handled

by our stores in France, representing the double handling of 50,500 tons of goods. During the retreat the Y.M.C.A. motor lorries became mobile centres of operation. They were filled up at the nearest stores available, and often travelled from eighty to ninety miles to a cross roads or convenient point where men going in and coming out of the line were provided with the necessary supplies. For the six months ending November 30, 1917, our free gifts to the troops in France amounted to £157,000. This figure does not include the cost of huts and equipment, nor yet the general expenditure on the work—but it embraces the cost of the hostels for the relatives of wounded, and free food and drink for the walking wounded and for the men serving in advanced positions.

*   *   *

A distinguished officer of the Danish Army called at the headquarters of the

British Y.M.C.A. after a visit to France, to acquaint himself with the history of our war work :—' One day I stood on Messines Ridge,' said he, ' and all around me was devastation caused by war, shells were to be seen bursting all around, accompanied by the deafening roar of the big guns. Overhead amidst the din could be heard the whirr of the engines of the German and Allied fighting machines. I felt thrilled to think I was in the midst of the greatest battle of history. Stepping aside a few yards I was surprised to find a dug-out with the Red Triangle sign. I could only exclaim, " What, these people here ! " '

* * *

One of the funniest sights we saw in France was that of a tiny British corporal marching behind ten stalwart German prisoners, escorting them back to their quarters after they had finished orderly duty in one of our tents. The humour of the situation evidently appealed to him, for he winked as he passed us—quite an unsoldierly thing to do !

*   *   *

Tommy has a knack of making himself comfortable, though his surroundings very often do not naturally suggest comfort. It is surprising what a snug bed and living room combined can be made out of a discarded hen-house ! A barn occupied by men of the Horse Guards Blue was ingeniously rigged up by its temporary tenants. One wall was missing and was made up with sacking—on the other side of this flimsy partition were the horses. The harness was hung round the walls, and four stakes driven into the ground for each bed. The wire that had bound hay bales had been ingeniously woven into wire mattresses stretched from stake to stake ; over it was stretched the sacking—also from hay bales—and over that again was a good thick layer of straw. There is never anything to be gained by grumbling, but everything by taking things cheerfully as they come and making the best of one's circumstances.

*   .   *   *

A Y.M.C.A. hut is a poor substitute for home, but our aim is to make every Y.M.C.A. as much like home as it is possible for it to be. It is surprising how much can be done by pictures, decorations and flowers, to give the home touch. A canary singing over the counter; a cat on the hearth; a bunch of primroses or forget-me-nots; a smile or a word of welcome; a woman's voice; a piano—family prayers at the close of the day—these are some of the things that count, and are numbered amongst the greatest assets of the Red Triangle.

*   *   *

It is strange how often scenes and sounds
of war and peace are intermingled. It is
a common sight to see men and women
going unconcernedly about their work,
and children playing in towns that are
habitually shelled or bombed. Stranger
still is it to note the habits of the wild
birds, constructing their nest amid scenes
of war and in localities subject to constant
bombardment. The Y.M.C.A. hut in
Ploegsteert Wood was destroyed during a
three hours' bombardment in May 1916,
but whenever there came a few seconds'
pause in the booming of the guns, the
nightingales sang as unconcernedly as in
the piping times of peace. We once
heard, near Hersin, a sort of duet between
a cuckoo and a big gun ; the bird punctu-
ating with its call the thunder of the guns,
and, as stated elsewhere, whilst the barrage
was in full swing the thrushes on Kemmel,
only a few hundred yards behind the guns,

sang as sweetly and merrily as in the lanes
and gardens of England. In the course of a
brief visit to the American front in France
we called at a little Y.M.C.A. shanty,
badly strafed, within a mile or so of the
enemy. Through the open window from
which all glass had long since vanished,
a swallow entered, and, perching on a
wire stretched across the room, carolled
joyously its simpl little song—a message
truly of peace and eternal hope !

*   *   *

The 'Walthamstow' hut at Remy had
to be temporarily abandoned during the
German offensive. The leader in charge
transferred operations to a dug-out across
the way, which adjoined a clearing station.
The inevitable caterer's boiler enabled him
to keep up a constant supply of hot tea
and coffee for the wounded. An Australian
terribly mutilated was brought in. A
happy smile, a few cheery words, and a

cup of steaming hot cocoa made the
Australian feel he had met a friend—and
speaking slowly, in a voice that was
scarcely louder than a whisper, he said,
' I wonder why I am allowed to suffer
like this.' ' I know why,' replied the
Y.M.C.A. man; 'you are suffering like this
so that two women I love—my mother and
my sister—may live in peace and safety
in the north of London. If it were not for
the sacrifices you and thousands of other
boys are making out here, that would be
impossible.'. The soldier lad was quiet
for some time, and then whispered to his
new-found friend—' I 'm glad to go on
suffering ! '

* * *

The same secretary tells an interesting
story of one of the bitter fights round
Passchendaele. The wounded were being
brought in on stretchers, and he was on
the spot with hot drinks for the boys.

The guns were quiet for a moment and a voice was heard singing clearly and distinctly :

> ' Lead, kindly Light, amid the encircling gloom,
>   Lead Thou me on.
> The night is dark, and I am far from home ;
>   Lead Thou me on !
> Keep Thou my feet ; I do not ask to see
> The distant scene ; one step enough for me.'

The singer was a private, badly wounded and being carried in on a stretcher. The subsequent verses were drowned in the roar of battle, but those standing round could see from the movement of the wounded man's lips that he was still singing. Thus it is possible for a man to find his Saviour near him even amid the horror and noise of war.

*   *   *

One day in 1917 we stood outside a little Y.M.C.A. at Erquinghem, lost during the German advance in the following spring, and standing there we heard ' Grandmother '

Y.M.C.A. MOTOR KITCHEN BEHIND THE LINES

INDIAN TROOPS AT THE SIGN OF THE RED TRIANGLE

speak. 'Grandmother,' it should be explained, was a mighty howitzer. It was
concealed under an improvised shed carefully camouflaged, and was brought out
on rails, in a horizontal position. As
we watched, it was brought to the vertical
and out shot a tongue of flame. The
projectile was so huge we could watch its
flight for miles until it disappeared from
view in the distance. Listening intently
we heard the explosion in the enemy's
lines. Many a Y.M.C.A. on the Western
Front is situated right amid the guns, and
when they are fired one knows it—
'Grandmother' speaking, seems to shake
the very foundations of the earth.

L

CHAPTER XIII

THE RED TRIANGLE IN THE EAST

The Y.M.C.A. is doing excellent work—its efforts are appreciated immensely by all ranks in this force. Experience of Y.M.C.A. work in the Army has long since convinced me how invaluable its services are to us, both in peace and war.—THE LATE LIEUT.-GENERAL SIR STANLEY MAUDE.

THE Macedonian call ' Come over and help us ' has been repeated in our own days, and has come from near and far East. The Red Triangle has been quick to respond to the call, and a few incidents of its work are recorded here, though the story itself must be told after the war. The Chief Executive officer of the Indian National Council is himself an Indian, and not only has he, with the assistance of his Council, been responsible for the great work of the Red Triangle in India, but also for the

162

extensive programme of work the Association has undertaken for Indian troops in East Africa, Mesopotamia, and Europe. In addition to work for British troops in India, the Y.M.C.A. has established work for Indian troops in a number of cantonments, where service parallel to that undertaken for British troops is carried on, with the exception that no religious work is done, unless in the case of Christian Sepoys.

The number of branches with British troops on August 1, 1917, was 43, worked by 40 European and American and 9 Indian secretaries, and 1 honorary lady secretary. With Indian troops there were 8 branches, worked by 1 European and 8 Indian secretaries. These figures do not include the temporary work undertaken by the Army Y.M.C.A. with the Waziristan Field Force, which terminated during August 1917, and which included 4 British and 4 Indian branches, with 3 European and 2 Indian secretaries. There was also 1 European secretary at Headquarters on August 1, 1917, for Army work in India ; and in addition secretaries engaged in civilian Y.M.C.A. work in several stations gave part of their time to Army work, as well as many voluntary workers.

In Burma a large barrack-room, made of wood and bamboo with a grass-thatched roof, houses the Association, which works amongst the men of the newly formed Burmese regiments. The whole building is on piles, and stands about six feet off the ground, thus preventing snakes and other unwelcome guests from coming inside. The regiments comprise not only Burmans but Karens, Chinese, and Arakanese. Most of the men are from the deep jungle, and very few of them can read or write. The gramophone interests them enormously, and they look inside it to see who is producing the sound, and will sit round in a circle listening to it for hours. Picture papers interest them, but usually they prefer holding the pictures upside down. The better educated men write a good deal on the free notepaper provided by the Y.M.C.A. Quartettes are sung by Karen and Chinese Christians. At the far end of the building is a huge image of the Buddha which was there before we came, and is used by some of the boys as a sort of chapel for private devotions. The boys have to take their choice between Christianity and Buddhism, and as we have three exceptionally good lamps there is much more light at the Y.M.C.A. end of the hall, and we have the better attendance in numbers at all events.

Egypt, handicapped at first through lack of money, has also done magnificently. There is no more important centre of Association activity in the world than the

Esbekia Gardens in Cairo. Ever since the
early days of the war, night after night,
thousands of khaki-clad warriors have
congregated in these lovely gardens, which
under other auspices might easily have
been one of the danger spots of Cairo,
instead of a kind of modern 'City of
Refuge' from the temptations of the city.
The Anzac hostel is another striking
feature of the work in Cairo. In June 1917
no fewer than 6893 soldiers slept in it,
and that was not by any means a record
month. The money for the purchase of
this hostel as the permanent property of
the Y.M.C.A. has been subscribed by
members of the Baltic, but the discovery
of the existence of a third mortgage has
delayed the completion of the purchase.
At Alexandria, Khartoum, Port Soudan,
on both sides of the canal and far into the
Sinai Peninsula, the Association outposts
have been busy. A Red Triangle hut in the

desert was destroyed by a bomb dropped from a hostile aeroplane, but when the smoke subsided the centre pole was still standing and the Association flag flying. The huts at Kantara are amongst the finest in the world, and neither here nor anywhere else has it been necessary to put up a notice intimating that the Y.M.C.A. is 'open to all.' Tommy knows it, and regards the Red Triangle as his own peculiar possession. One cannot conceive of any place on earth where it is more needed than in one of these desert camps, where there is nothing to do, nowhere to go, and nothing to see but endless stretches of monotonous and dreary sand. Under such circumstances the Red Triangle is Tommy's tuck shop ; his church—with the chaplain as the parson ; his post-office, concert hall, social room, school, and home. This is true of every fighting front, and that is why the Association has won for itself a lasting place in the affections of the manhood of the Empire.

A young soldier writing home the day after his arrival in Mesopotamia, said the first thing he struck on landing was the welcome sign of the Red Triangle. ' And,' said he, ' if we are ordered next to the North Pole, I am sure we shall find it there !' The Y.M.C.A. secretary for Mesopotamia tells of a visit he paid to a centre on the way to Bagdad. It was a big bare marquee, crammed with men, with very little furniture in it—the difficulties of transport being so great in those days—just half a dozen tables and a few chairs, a heap of books, and a number of games. There were six inches of dust all over the floor, and the temperature was 120 degrees in the shade, yet one thing that attracted the men to the Y.M.C.A. marquee was that it enabled them to escape the heat of their own bell tents.

Through the kindness of Sir Alfred Yarrow a Red Triangle motor launch has since then been provided for use on the Tigris, and has greatly simplified transport. The central Y.M.C.A. at Bagdad is one of the best of our war buildings, and is situated on the banks of the Tigris. An Association centre has been established on the reputed site of the Garden of Eden.

*   *   *

The story of the Red Triangle in Palestine is an epic in itself. For months the Association occupied dug-outs along the Palestine front, and in those days one secretary devoted the whole of his time to making personal purchases for officers and men, who could not themselves get away to any centre of civilisation to make purchases on their own account. Gaza was the first centre occupied in the Holy Land ; Beersheba, Jaffa, and Jerusalem being occupied later. At Jaffa the former German

Consulate was fitted up as a Y.M.C.A., and the Red Triangle as a matter of course has made its appearance on a big building in Jerusalem.

Malta was a very important centre in the early days of the war, and the Y.M.C.A. flourished in its numerous hospital camps. In Macedonia the work has been difficult, but greatly appreciated in Salonica itself, as well as on the Varda and the Struma. The need has been urgent, and every effort has been made to meet that need. Transport difficulties have led to inevitable delays in the delivery of stores and equipment, but there are more than forty centres now, including five for Serbian soldiers.

The Y.M.C.A. had its part in the ill-fated expedition to the Dardanelles. Mudros, Imbros, and Tenedos were centres of importance in those days, and the Red Triangle was at work in each island.

The urgent need of the troops was for soft drinks, and those ordinary canteen supplies that give variety to the soldiers' menu, and make the official rations palatable. The official canteens were powerless to meet the demand. We were anxious to help, but transport was the difficulty. At last, through the kindness of Lord Nunburn-hólme, we were enabled to charter the s.s. *Nero* of the Wilson Line, and despatch it with a cargo of canteen supplies to the value of eleven thousand pounds to Mudros. A few days later the Peninsula was evacuated, but whilst they were there the men availed themselves to the full of the opportunity of buying supplementary food at British prices. When the *Nero* reached Mudros, Greek venders were selling our Tommies tinned fruit at twelve shillings a tin, and other prices were correspondingly high.

In the centre of an official photograph

of Anzac showing the Bay, the camp, and the surrounding sandhills, are to be seen the letters ' Y.M.C.A.' They appear on a tiny marquee and close to it a big dug-out, measuring 30 by 19 feet, in which the Red Triangle carried through its programme of friendliness and good cheer, always under shell-fire. One night a fragment of a Turkish shell, weighing twelve and a half pounds, found its way through the roof of that dug-out. At Cape Helles there were three tiny tents fastened end on end. Had they been larger they could scarcely have escaped the attention of ' Asiatic Annie,' the big Turkish gun that dominated the position. As it was, the Officer Commanding the advanced base at Lancashire Landing wrote to Headquarters to say how much the men appreciated those tents, and explained that the previous day an eight-inch high explosive shell from a Turkish gun had burst in the centre of the

middle tent and completely destroyed it.
'Fortunately,' said he, 'it didn't damage
the piano, and still more fortunately,' he
added, 'it didn't harm the gramophone.'
That was curious, and we thought of some
of the gramophones we had known, and
felt it would have been no disaster if a
shell had destroyed the lot ! This gramophone was different, however, for it had
only just been wound up when the shell
burst, but regardless of the bustle and
confusion caused by the explosion, it kept
on playing until it had finished the last
note of the tune! What a splendid object
lesson for the Allies, to stick to the job
they have on hand to the finish, or in
other words, till victory crowns their
efforts. Many months after the incident
here recorded the Irish Y.M.C.A. was
invited to open up at Rathdrum. The
secretary responsible interviewed the O.C.,
and learning that he was a Catholic,

asked politely if he knew the work of the Y.M.C.A. 'Indeed I do,' was the reply. 'I was at Cape Helles when a shell burst in your tent. I was the officer in charge, and it was my duty to remove casualties. I went up to the tents fearing the worst, and shall never forget the smiling face of the Y.M.C.A. man behind the counter. It won me over completely.'

A distinguished officer wrote :—

'Your work has been of inestimable value to the troops, filling a gap which it is impossible for the Military Authorities to provide for. "Always first up, always working hard, and always welcome—the Red Triangle will always be gratefully remembered by the soldiers in the Great War." '

CHAPTER XIV

SIDE LINES OF THE RED TRIANGLE

The Y.M.C.A. has fashioned a girdle of mercy and loving-kindness round the world which will stand to their credit as long as the memory of this war exists.—LORD CURZON OF KEDLESTON.

THERE are numerous side-lines to this work, that are important enough in themselves, the significance of which is scarcely realised by the general public, or even by those who are supporting the movement. Take, for example, the 'Snapshots from Home' movement, which represented the combined voluntary work of the photographers of the United Kingdom, organised under the Red Triangle. Upwards of 650,000 snapshots were sent out to soldiers and sailors on active service, each one bearing a message of love and a reminder of home. Sir Evelyn Wood, V.C., was one of the first to recognise the significance of the letter-writing that is done on such a large scale in the Y.M.C.A. tents. The veteran Field-Marshal pointed out that the benefit was two-fold: first, it occupied the time of the men; and, secondly, it kept them in touch with their homes, both matters of first importance. 'That's what my Dad always puts on his letters to Mummy,' said a little girl, pointing to the Red Triangle on the notepaper, when on a visit to the Crystal Palace. Fifteen to twenty million pieces of stationery are distributed free of charge to the troops monthly by the Y.M.C.A., and in four years the total issued amounted to upwards of nine hundred million pieces. Workers are often called upon to write letters for the men, and the latter make all sorts of mistakes with their correspondence. Sometimes they stamp their letters but

A SHAKEDOWN IN A LONDON HUT

RELATIVES OF THE DANGEROUSLY WOUNDED ARE LOOKED AFTER
BY THE Y.M.C.A. IN FRANCE

Y.M.C.A. NIGHT MOTOR TRANSPORT

forget to address them, often they address them but forget the stamps. One lad was greatly excited and wanted the secretary in charge of the post-office to rescue two letters he had posted earlier in the afternoon. When asked why he wanted them back he blushed like a schoolgirl and stammered out, 'I 've written two letters —one to my mother and the other to my sweetheart—and I 've put them in the wrong envelopes!' The letters were not rescued, for more than five thousand had been posted before he discovered his mistake, and one wonders what happened!

*   *   *

In Paris the Association has established a central inquiry bureau under the Hôtel Édouard VII. off the Grand Boulevard. Two daily excursions are arranged around Paris, and two each week to Versailles. Representatives of the Red Triangle meet all the principal trains, day and night.

M

The Hôtel Florida is now run under the Association for British troops, whilst the American Y.M.C.A. has its Headquarters for France in the city, and has taken over several large hotels and other buildings.

There is not the romance about the work of the Red Triangle in the munition areas, that there is in what it is doing for our fighting men, but there can be no doubt as to its importance. The munition workers as a class are as patriotic as any other class, but their work is drab, monotonous, and strenuous. Little has been done officially to bring home to the man who makes the shell the relationship of his work to the man who fires it ; or of the woman who works on the aeroplane to the man who is to fly in it, and yet the one can do nothing without the other. Things have changed for the better, but earlier in the war the output of munitions was positively hindered by the inadequacy of the canteen facilities available to the munition workers. The Y.M.C.A. was the first organisation to attempt to meet this need on anything like a large scale, and eventually the work grew to considerable dimensions. Our work in the munition areas has been essentially a ladies' movement, and has largely consisted of canteen work. Other features are being increasingly added, music and singing have been organised successfully, lectures have been greatly appreciated, and several big athletic features introduced. Sporting events, also cricket and football leagues for munition workers, have been well supported. It is intensely interesting to see these people at work, and no other proof of British organising power and ability are necessary than a visit to some of the great works, many of which were not built for the purpose of manufacturing munitions of war, and others improvised since the commencement of hostilities. At one place in which a canteen was formally opened by Princess Helena Victoria—who has taken the keenest interest in the development of our munitions department—from ordinary. shipbuilding before the war great changes had taken place : a Super-Dreadnought was approaching completion ; several T.B.D.'s were on the stocks, and some of the latest type of submarines were being built ; aeroplanes were being turned out at an incredible rate ; shells made by the thousand ; rigid air-ships were under construction ; and, perhaps as wonderful as anything, artificial feet were being made in the same workshops.

*   *   *

Incidentally might be mentioned here, the work the Association is doing for officers. There are four large hostels in London for the accommodation of officers, and one for officer-cadets. The young officer is often not blessed with too much of this world's goods, and hotel life is expensive, and not always too comfortable. The success of these hostels has demonstrated the need. At Havre, Calais, St. Omer, Étaples, and many centres up the line, as well as in home camps, such as Ripon, we have the pleasure of doing something to serve the officer, and in many English camps we have opened huts for the exclusive use of officer-cadets. Gidea Park, Berkhampstead, and Denham were amongst. the first and most successful of these centres. The interned officers in Switzerland and Holland are largely catered for by the Y.M.C.A.

*   *   *

It has been a pleasure to co-operate from time to time with the work of the R.A.M.C. and the Red Cross. In huts, in hospitals, and convalescent camps, in caring for the relatives of wounded, in work for the walking wounded, and in many other ways the Red Cross and the Red Triangle have worked closely together. An officer of the R.A.M.C. (T.), has written the following interesting description of the work of the Y.M.C.A. for the walking wounded :—' The O.C. the Divisional Walking Wounded Collecting Post was frankly worried as he sat in his tiny sandbagged hut with the D.A.D.M.S., and talked over all the problems which faced him in view of the "stunt" due to come off at dawn a few days later. "I've got plenty of dressings, and everything of that sort," he said, "and, of course, I can get plenty more brought up by returning ambulance cars. But there is the question of food—there's the rub. The numbers of wounded vary so greatly, and it's not so easy to lay in a huge reserve of grub as it is of dressings. Of course, I've done my best, but I'm rather worried." "If that is all your worry we'll soon put that right," answered the optimist of the staff. "We'll get the Y.M.C.A. chap on the job." "What can he do?" "What can he not do rather? You wait and see. Come along and we'll call on him now."

' In a little shed of corrugated iron by the side of a shell-swept road they found him. With his coat off and his sleeves rolled up, he was pushing across the counter steaming mugs of cocoa and piles of buns to the crowd of hungry and clamouring Tommies who besieged his premises. He was not a young man. Not the strongest-hearted of Medical Boards would have passed him for service. To put it briefly, he had no right in the world to be where he was, in one of the nastiest corners of that particularly nasty place, Flanders. But there he was, roughing it with the rest of them, and to judge from his smiling countenance, thoroughly enjoying every particle of his experience. "Hello, Major!" he called out cheerfully on seeing his two officer visitors. "Anything I can do for you to-day?" "Rather! A whole lot. Can we have a talk in your own place—away from the crowd?" The Y.M.C.A. man led the way to the six feet square hole in the ground which he called his billet, and there the medical staff officer explained his needs. "There's a stunt on in a few days," he said. "You may have guessed that. What can you do to help us? You know the pressure under which the R.A.M.C. will be working. It'll be a big job dressing all the casualties there are likely to be; but we'll manage that bit. What we want is a hand in the feeding of them. You understand?" The face of the secretary glowed with excitement. "I'll do any mortal thing I can," he answered eagerly. "There'll be nothing doing here once the show starts, so I'll shut down, and bring my whole stock over to your dressing station, and my staff too. We can feed several hundred if you 'll let us." " What about the cost of the grub ? " " Not a word about cost, sir ! You 're welcome to it free, gratis, and for nothing, with all the pleasure in the world." " Thanks awfully," said the D.A.D.M.S. " That 's just what I wanted you to offer, and I thought you would ; your folks have helped us so often before." " Jolly good job," mused the Y.M.C.A. man, " that I have kept hidden those extra cases of chocolates and sweet biscuits. I thought there might be something of this sort coming off."

'Ere the grey dawn of a certain morning brought the nerve-racking inferno of barrage and counter-barrage, the entire stock of the canteen was installed in the larger of the two huts which formed the collecting post. Boxes of biscuits, chocolates, and cigarettes with the lids knocked off, stood ranged along the wall, ready for the tired and hungry guests who would soon appear. Outside, in two huge cauldrons, gallons of strong cocoa were brewing merrily. Little was spoken by the men standing around, as they waited, nerves a trifle on edge, for the breaking of the storm. Suddenly from somewhere in the rear came the hollow boom of a "heavy," the artillery signal, and in an instant every battery in the area had hurled its first salvo of the barrage. The air was full of noise, the rolling roar of the guns at " drum fire," the hissing and screaming of flying shells, the echoes of far-away explosions. The ground trembled as if an earthquake had come. The battle had begun.

'The O.C. looked in at the door of the hut. "Everything ready?" he asked. "Ready and waiting," answered the Y.M.C.A. man, and very soon in twos and threes the wounded began to dribble in, and shortly a steady stream of battered humanity was straggling down the road, to halt at the welcome sight of the hut with the Red Cross flag by its door. How some of them limped over every weary step of the way was beyond understanding. With shattered limbs and mangled flesh they came, worn, hungry, thirsty, in agony, some stumbling alone, some helped along by less grievously injured comrades. In a pitiful throng they gathered around the dressing station.

'The quick eyes of the R.A.M.C. sergeant picked out the worst cases, and these were hurried into the hut where the medical officers plied their sorrowful trade. The others sat down and waited their turn with the stolid patience of the British soldier when he is wounded, and among them worked an Angel of Mercy, an elderly angel clad in a flannel shirt, and a pair of mud-stained khaki trousers. Amid the poor jetsam of the fight went the Y.M.C.A. man with his mugs of cocoa and his biscuits, his chocolate and his cigarettes, as much a minister of healing as was the surgeon with his dressings and anodynes. All the men were bitterly cold after their long night of waiting in the old front trench, or were dead beat with the nervous strain of the action and the pain of their wounds. All were hungry. A few no longer cared greatly what more might happen to them, for they had reached the limit of endurance, as surely as they had reached the limit of suffering. But even to those last the warm drink and the food and, perhaps more than anything else, the soothing nicotine, brought back life and hope in place of apathy and despair. 'God bless you, sir,' murmured a man here and there. But the greater part could find no words

to speak the gratitude which their eyes
told forth so clearly.'

This little story is not the tale of one
actual incident. It is only the stereotype
of scenes that have been acted and re-
acted often and often at the Front. Time
and time again has the Red Triangle come
to the aid of the Red Cross, placing its
workers and its stores unreservedly at the
disposal of the Royal Army Medical Corps.
When the wounded have been pouring into
the dressing stations in hundreds, the
Y.M.C.A. workers have taken over the
responsibility of feeding them, and have
halved the cares of the overwrought
R.A.M.C. This they have done not once
but unnumbered times, and what gratitude
they have earned from their guests ! The
wounded man can scarcely realise what he
owes to the surgeon who tends his injuries ;
but he does appreciate his debt to the man
who feeds him and gives him the ' fag '

for which he has been craving.   The cocoa and cigarettes of the Y.M.C.A. do not figure among the ' medicaments of the Pharmacopœia, yet many a ' walking wounded ' will swear to you that they have saved his life — as perhaps they have.

CHAPTER XV

THE RED TRIANGLE AND THE WHITE ENSIGN

Surely the Almighty God does not intend this war to be just a hideous fracas, a bloody, drunken orgy. There must be purpose in it all ; improvement must be born out of it. In what direction ? France has already shown us the way, and has risen out of her ruined cities with a revival of religion that is most wonderful. England still remains to be dug out of the stupor of self-satisfaction and complacency which the great and flourishing condition has steeped her in. And until she can be stirred out of this condition, until a religious revival takes place at home, just so long will the war continue. When she can look on the future with humbler eyes and a prayer on her lips, then we can begin to count the days towards the end.—ADMIRAL SIR DAVID BEATTY, K.C.B., M.V.O., D.S.O., K.C.V.O.

THIS chapter is written in a 'sleeper' at the close of a busy day in the North. The day has been made a memorable one by a visit to the *Queen Elizabeth*, as she lay at her moorings in one of our great naval bases. She is one of the greatest instruments of war in the world, and it was a revelation to enter one of the gun turrets of the super-dreadnought, to look through the periscope, or see the ingenious mechanism that moved those mighty guns, and lifts into position the huge projectile that is capable of delivering death and destruction to an enemy many miles away. It was more than interesting to visit the wireless rooms, where ceaseless watch is kept by day and night, and to see the wonderful orderliness of everything, and to note that every one on board was ready, and their only fear that the German Fleet might never be tempted out again. The visit to the *Queen Elizabeth* left one thinking of the service the Red Triangle has been able to render to the White Ensign. During the war there are not as many opportunities for work amongst naval men as in peace time, but there is all the more need that

Y.M.C.A. IN THE FRONT-LINE DUG-OUTS ON THE PALESTINE FRONT

Y.M.C.A. DUG-OUT AND CANTEEN ON PALESTINE FRONT

when the men are ashore everything that is possible should be done for them. The Scottish National Council have up-to-date well-equipped hostels and recreation-rooms in several naval centres, and those at Edinburgh and Glasgow are thronged with bluejackets. South of the Border there are many fine hostels and recreation-rooms for sailors, and in scores of centres in England, Wales, and Ireland the Red Triangle is catering successfully for the needs of our bluejackets. The biggest crowd of all is to be found in the quarters occupied by the Y.M.C.A. at the Crystal Palace, where thousands of men every day use the Y.M.C.A. as their club, and find in it their home. We shall never know all we owe to our splendid Navy, and that debt can never be fully paid. At the close of the war we are planning to erect permanent hostels and institutes for sailors in several naval bases at home and in some of the

N

great foreign stations. Much appreciated war work for sailors is being carried on now at Brindisi and Taranto, for the men of the drifters employed on minesweeping in the Mediterranean, also at Malta, Mudros, and other centres overseas.

A demand for a Y.M.C.A. on a battleship came from the men of H.M.S. *Conqueror*, and it has been found most helpful.

Many isolated naval stations round the British coast are supplied with cabinets, each one containing a gramophone, library, a supply of writing materials, and games. For obvious reasons it would be imprudent whilst the war is on to indicate the centres by name in which the Red Triangle is serving the men of the Navy, but there will be a great story to tell when the war is over.

CHAPTER XVI

THE RELIGION OF THE RED TRIANGLE

> The work of the Y.M.C.A. is, to my mind, one of the outstanding features of this war. Their efforts, along with other agencies working for the highest welfare of the Army, have shown a true catholic spirit, and made it easier for our soldiers to live a noble, true and clean life. May God's blessing follow their increasing influence.—THE CHAPLAIN-GENERAL TO THE FORCES.

> The Y.M.C.A. has been one of the really great things which have come into their own in this world crisis. It has been a Hindenburg Line of the Christian faith.—DR. MICHAEL SADLER, VICE-CHANCELLOR OF LEEDS UNIVERSITY.

THE Y.M.C.A. is not in camp as a rival to the ordinary Church organisations, nor yet to supplant or in any conceivable way to undermine the influence of the chaplains. Its large and commodious huts and tents have been used in thousands of camps for the official Church Parade services, and in many cases there has been no other suitable

room available. We have counted it a
privilege on Sunday mornings to place our
equipment unreservedly at the disposal of
all the official chaplains who desired to use
it. We have welcomed the opportunity
of assisting the great and important work
the chaplains are doing for the men of His
Majesty's Forces, for the Y.M.C.A. is itself
a wing of the great Christian army, and has
sometimes been described as the Church
in action.   Apart from the support in men
and money it has received from members
of the Churches, the war work of the Red
Triangle would have been impossible.   The
Y.M.C.A. is not a church, and will never
become one.   It administers no sacraments,
its membership is confined to one sex ; it
discourages in all its branches the holding
of meetings that clash with those of the
Churches, and in every possible way each
member unattached is encouraged to join
the Church of his choice.

In the course of a striking letter to *The Challenge* of July 12, 1918, a correspondent said :—' We turn, for an example, to the Y.M.C.A. Conceal the unpleasant truth how we may, the outstanding religious performance of this war in the eyes of the public at large has not been the daily services in Church—not even the Holy Communion—but the work done in the Y.M.C.A. huts. It is along those lines that we must travel if we are to win the world. For the mediævally-minded, for the intellectually timid, there is always Rome. But it is not by those that the new England will be built, and it is the new England we must save for Christ.'

Another writer to the same Anglican journal said it had been stated that ' after the war there would be a holy Roman Church and a holy Y.M.C.A., but no more Church of England.' The fact of the matter is the Y.M.C.A. is not making the work of the Churches unnecessary, but rather it is giving the ordinary man a new conception of what Christianity really is, and is thus helping to interpret the churches to the masses, and is acting as a bridge or a communication trench between the organised forces of Christianity in the front line, so to speak, and the great masses away back in reserve, on which they desire to draw. Some people have spoken sneeringly of 'canteen religion'; the soldier never does—and why should he? There is nothing new about it, for it is as old as the early days of Christianity, only the gospel of the 'cup of cold water' has been adapted to the needs of modern warfare, so that the man in the firing-line knows it from experience as the gospel of the 'cup of hot coffee.' Straggling back to a clearing station, wounded, plastered with mud, and racked with pain, the most eloquent of sermons would not help him, but a hot drink, a few biscuits or even a cigarette, if given in the name of the Master may put new heart and life into him, and give him fresh courage for the way. The Churches realise this, and have given us of their best as far as helpers are concerned.

We have a vivid recollection of visiting the big Y.M.C.A. hut in the Cavalry Camp at Rouen in 1915. It was the ordinary week-night service, and more than six hundred men were present. A famous Scottish preacher had conducted the service, and at the close we chatted with him for a few minutes in the quiet room. 'Before I came out to France,' said he, 'I knew you had a great opportunity. Now I know that the greatest spiritual opportunity in history rests on your shoulders—is with the Y.M.C.A.' And yet there is a way of doing spiritual work that would make all spiritual work in camp absolutely impossible. We remember visiting a big

hut one day—it did not sport the Red
Triangle, but was beautifully furnished.
Over the door was a bold device ' A Home
from Home ! All Welcome ! ' On entering, the first thing one saw was the text
' Behold your sins will find you out ! '
And a few yards further on ' The wages
of sin is death.' ' No smoking ! ' was
another notice, and yet another, ' This
hut will be closed every evening from seven
to eight for a gospel service.' Religion
to appeal to the soldier must be natural
and not forced, and must be free from
controversy and unreality. The British
soldier hates a sham, and instinctively
classes the hypocrite with the Hun. He
may not understand our Shibboleths ; he
has no use for our controversies, but he
can and does understand the Life of the
Master, when he sees the beauty of that
Life reflected in some humble follower of
His, who day by day is risking his life at

the Front, that he may supply a cup of cocoa to a wounded soldier, or who is slaving behind a Y.M.C.A. refreshment counter at home, and doing uncongenial work for the love of Christ.

* * *

When it was decided to send the Indian troops to France, the Y.M.C.A. offered its services to the Indian Government. The offer was refused. At last, however, permission was given to supply recreation marquees for the use of the Indian Army in France, but only on condition that there should be no proselytising, no preaching, no prayers, no hymn singing, no Testaments or Bibles given, and no tracts. The Y.M.C.A. accepted the conditions, and though some of its friends felt it meant lowering the flag, it has loyally kept its promise, and most people realise to-day that this was one of the greatest pieces of Christian strategy of our times. A visit to one of the

Red Triangle huts or tents in an Indian camp is a revelation. You hear the Mohammedan call to prayer, see the tiny mosque, and realise in how many and varied ways it is possible for the Y.M.C.A. to be of service to these brave men of another faith. A professor reported at one of the big base camps as a worker. He had come to lecture to the troops, and when asked by the leader as to his subjects replied, 'Sanscrit and Arabic.' The leader wondered how on earth he could make use of a man as a lecturer to British Tommies, who only lectured on those two obscure and difficult topics. The professor found his niche, however, teaching the Mohammedan priest to read his Koran — the leader commenting — 'The more he knows it, the less he will trust it.'

It is interesting to note how well these Indian heroes get on with our own Tommies.

They play their games and sometimes sing their songs. When. 'Tipperary' was all the rage, the Indians had their own version of the chorus, which they sang with great enthusiasm.   It ran thus :

'Bura dur hai Tipperary,
Bura dur hai kouch ho,
Bura dur hai Tipperary,
    Sukipas powncheniko,
Ram, ram, Piccadilly,
Salam Leicester Square.
Bura, bura dur hai Tipperary,
    Likem dil hoa pus ghai.'

On one occasion the secretary of an important base said he had arranged a new stunt for us that evening—the formal opening of a hut in the Indian Cavalry Hospital Camp. We arrived to find the hut crowded, and a great banquet arranged in our honour. Nothing need be said as to the banquet or its disastrous results as far as we are concerned! The Indians enjoyed it, and that was the important thing.

Before the banquet we had the privilege
of greeting the men and welcoming them
to the Y.M.C.A., and after we had finished,
the leading Mohammedan in the camp
mounted the platform and gave a great
oration in honour of the Christian Association. He was followed by the leading
Brahmin, and he in turn by the senior
Sheik, all speaking in most cordial terms of
the Y.M.C.A.   In the midst of the orations,
a stately Indian advanced solemnly and
placed a garland of flowers round my neck.
Thrice this garlanding process was repeated
on different occasions—lovely roses and
sweet peas—and it was a great and much
appreciated honour, though it made one
feel a trifle foolish at the time.   After the
banquet we proceeded to the adjoining
recreation tent, and it was an inspiration to
see it crammed from end to end with men
of many religions and different races, all
happy and contented and all usefully

employed. On the platform a ' budginee'
or Indian concert was proceeding; a
crowd of men at the tables were learning
to write ; another crowd receiving a lesson
in English ; a large group looking at
pictures and illustrated magazines, whilst
others were playing games or listening
enraptured to the strains of the Indian
records on the gramophone. The C.O.
who took us round, said that when the
men came to France not one of them could
even sign his name to his pay book, they
all had to do it by means of thumb-prints.
' To-day,' said he, ' every man can sign
his name, and many can write an intelligent
letter, and they have learned everything in
the Y.M.C.A.' A few days previously an
Indian of some rank stood with folded
arms, his back against the wall, in that very
tent. He said nothing, but took in everything, and when the marquee closed for
the night and the dusky hero warriors

retired to their tents, he spoke to the Indian secretary in charge. ' I have watched you men,' said he; 'you are not paid by the Government, you come when you like and you go when you like. There is only one religion in the world that would send its servants to do what you are doing—to serve and not to proselytise. When this war is over and we return to India, I want you to send one of your men to my village. My people are all Hindus, but they will do what I tell them. I have been watching you carefully, and I have come to the conclusion that Christianity will fit the East as it can never fit the West.' One of the lessons of the Red Triangle is that you can never win men by antagonising them, or by speaking disrespectfully of the things they hold dear. Love must ever be the conqueror, and the love of all loves is the love of God revealed in His Son, Jesus Christ.

*   *   *

Our Jewish friends were surprised and delighted in the dark days at the close of 1914, to find that the doors of the Y.M.C.A. were thrown widely open to their padres, who could gather in soldiers of their community to worship God in their own way in the huts of the Red Triangle. They have not been slow to show their appreciation—several Y.M.C.A. huts have been given officially by Jews ; one well-known and much used hostel bears the name ' Jewish Y.M.C.A.,' and Jewish padres will go to any trouble or inconvenience to help our work at home or overseas. No Red Triangle hut can be used for proselytising by Catholic, Protestant, Moslem, or Jew— that goes without saying—but any official chaplain is welcome to the use of our huts for instructing his own people in their own faith.

A striking article recently appeared in a Catholic journal, from which we cull the following paragraphs, expressing as they do another point of view :—

'"R.C.," "C. of E.," "Y.M.C.A."—these three are the religions of the Front. The drumhead service, whilst nominally "C. of E.," is, of course, more a military parade than a religious function. It is not without a certain amount of picturesque Army ceremonial, but to the Catholic soldier, as a Catholic, the spectacle is an uninteresting one. The Y.M.C.A., too, I think, would not claim to be a religion. It is perhaps a religious institution ; a kind of spiritual ration-dump. Its huts, even during a cinema show, and at the counters where they sell Woodbines and chocolates, have a Christianised atmosphere. No soldier fears to be thought "too good" through attending a Y.M.C.A. service. That is, perhaps, where its undoubtedly great influence comes in. It gives the impression, one supposes, to these soldiers that here they have what the P.S.A. fraternity call "a man's religion for man." It caters for the frequent English soul which (perhaps in the Charity of God) finds a path to Heaven in the singing of second-rate hymns on Sunday evening ; in the constant repetition of "Abide with me," and "O God, our help in ages past."

THE Y.M.C.A. AT BASRA, MESOPOTAMIA

THE CENTRAL Y.M.C.A., BAGHDAD

It is difficult to say if the influence of the Y.M.C.A. is much responsible for the remarkably even, and considering all things, somewhat high moral code of the Army out here. Rather, perhaps (Deo gratias), it is an English heritage from the past. Most emphatically one cannot help being struck by the excellent moral lives that many of these men live, when all things are considered. Of course, to a large extent, there is the lack of occasions of sin. Drunkenness, most possibly, is rare because the authorities have greatly restricted, and wisely, the hours of drinking, and the beer, etc., available, even if taken in large quantities, is rarely intoxicating. Frankly, it appears that the good influence of the Y.M.C.A. is derived from the temporal comforts and conveniences it offers to the much-tried B.E.F. men. I stood outside a Y.M.C.A. building one night, in the worst of weather, weather as foul as it can be in France in war time. Three rain-sodden Canadian infantrymen trudged along towards the place, and their ears caught the sound of some execrable piano-strumming. "Holy Hell," said one, "there's some music there; come on!" That is the story, in epitome, of the Y.M.C.A. In the mercy of God, it is a good one."

*   *   *

A young soldier sent to an English paper the following interesting account of a Communion Service held in one of our huts at the Front :—

'The following Tuesday, just as our company was going " up the line " to the trenches, a Communion service was held in the rest-room of the Y.M.C.A. hut. I attended it along with nine other men, and the service was conducted by a well-known Scottish Y.M.C.A. worker, who at the time was acting as the leader of the hut. In that little room we ten men in khaki were verily in the presence of the Unseen. I never realised Christ to be so near as when we handled the elements. For myself I can truly say that, in the grey dawn of the following morning, I went up to meet the enemy with a strange peace, and a deep assurance in my soul that, come what might, I need fear no evil, knowing that He was with me—and so it proved to be. Our time in the trenches was the most exciting I have yet experienced, but He kept near, and so " all 's well." '

CHAPTER XVII

STORIES OF THE INVERTED TRIANGLE

I am sending you a pound note, the first I ever received, as I am a poor old woman not able to work. To maintain my home I used to take in washing, but now I cannot even do my own, but the other Sunday, when I shook hands with one that I used to wash for, he put that bit of paper in my hand, but said nothing, so I received it as part payment for work done over seven years ago, and when I looked at it, I thanked God, and said I would give it to some good cause, and I think I cannot do better than help you to get shelter for the soldiers. God bless 'em.

MORE than five hundred thousand men have signed the War Roll pledge of allegiance to our Lord Jesus Christ, which has now been formally adopted by the Churches, and which reads as follows :

'I hereby pledge my allegiance to the Lord Jesus Christ, as my Saviour and King, and by God's help will fight

His battles for the Victory of His Kingdom.'

Many have no doubt forgotten their promise, but for many it has meant the beginning of a new life, and to thousands of parents the knowledge that the boy, who was their all, signed this declaration before making the supreme sacrifice, has brought untold comfort.

Wherever practicable a Quiet Room for prayer and Bible study is included in our camp outfit, also a book-stall for Testaments, pledge cards, and religious literature. Millions of Testaments and gospel portions have been distributed free of charge, and realising the difficulty of obtaining gospel booklets or tracts that appeal to men, a new one from the pen of the General Secretary was issued each of the first thirty weeks of the war. The approved plan has been to have family prayers, no matter how brief, as far as practicable in every hut, every night, and if this feature of the programme is not popular, the fault is usually to be found in the one who leads.

A casual observer, after visiting a Y.M.C.A. hut, sometimes comes to the conclusion that the Association is doing a great social work, but is not much as a religious force. It is not difficult to understand that point of view. He has seen two or three hundred men clamouring at the refreshment counter for coffee, buns or cigarettes ; the billiard tables have been fully occupied ; hundreds of soldiers were writing letters at the tables provided for the purpose, and hundreds joining in some rowdy chorus, or heartily laughing at a humorous song or funny sketch. Where then does the spiritual work of the Red Triangle come in ? The best answer is to quote what has actually happened.

To the south-west of Salisbury Plain

there was before the war a tiny village. To-day it is the centre of a big camp, which, incidentally, contains several Y.M.C.A. huts. The leader of No. 4 was talking to the Church of England padre one morning. They were warm friends and the chaplain was frank in his remarks : ' I think you are overdoing it,' said he, ' by having prayers in the hut every night. Surely it would be better,' he added, ' if you concentrated on one evening of the week instead.' ' I have thought and prayed about it,' replied the leader, ' and it is a matter of principle with me. These dear boys are all going to the Front next week, and no matter what the programme of the day, I feel we ought to finish at night with a public acknowledgment of God.' ' Very good,' replied the padre, .' if that is your conviction, carry on ! Take prayers yourself this evening.' And he did. He was no orator ; he was not a college man, neither was he ordained. It was a simple little service, and did not take more than ten or fifteen minutes from start to finish. There was an opening hymn, one of the old familiar ones, that took the lads away back to the homes of their childhood. A short passage of scripture was read, followed by a few straight but sympathetic words of exhortation and a brief closing prayer. That was all, and the same thing, no doubt, took place in hundreds of centres the same night. Prayers over and the 'King' sung, the leader came down from the platform, where a young private greeted him and shook his hand till it hurt saying, 'I want to thank you for giving me a new vision of a God I once knew.' Walking towards the centre of the hall, a young subaltern greeted him saying, 'I want to thank you for that little service; it has been no end of a help to me, and I should like to give you this for your work,' so saying he handed him an envelope, and looking inside he found a letter from the lieutenant's mother, containing thirty shillings in postal orders to be spent by him in camp. The service had helped him, and that was his thankoffering. The hut cleared, the men retired for the night to their sleeping quarters. A solitary soldier lingered by the doorway as if he wanted some one to speak to him. 'Good-night, my lad,' said the leader, ' can I do anything for you?' Instead of replying the soldier burst out crying, and later said, 'If you will you can save me from a great crime!' 'Save you from a crime—whatever do you mean?' And then the trooper told his story. There was nothing uncommon about it. He and his brother had made love to the same girl, their mother had intervened, ' and,' he said, ' I have written to my mother this evening a letter that no boy should write to his mother, and after attending your service to-night, I feel I would give all I 've got to take back that letter ! ' The letter was found and destroyed, and the soldier rejoiced in what he regarded as a great deliverance. This is no story of an orthodox revival, but of the kind of thing that may be taking place hundreds of times any week.

*   *   *

In the early days the famous ———— Division assembled in one of the great camps near Winchester. Regiments and units were there from India, South Africa— from all parts of the world. Rain came down in torrents and the mud was appalling. The huge Red Triangle tents were crowded from morning till night and the devoted workers, all too few in number, had neither time nor strength for religious work in the ordinary acceptance of the term. They could have limited their canteen work, and closed the refreshment

counter excepting for a few hours daily.
That would have been the easier plan,
and would have given them the opportunity of devoting themselves to concerts
and meetings in the evenings. The alternative would have been to spend and be
spent in serving the material needs of the
men, trusting that God would use the
atmosphere of the place and the personal
contact of the workers to influence the
men, and thus make up for their inability
to do much in the meeting line. They
chose the latter plan, and the leader
retiring for the night would throw himself
on his bed and sometimes fall asleep
without undressing. At times suffering
from the reaction, he would ask himself
the question, ' Is it worth while ? Am I
doing the right thing ? ' The answer came
the night before the men left for the Front.
It had been a record day, every moment
had been crowded, and they had sold out.

The majority had retired for the night, a few remained to tidy up the tents. This task accomplished, a group of soldiers gathered round the leader, and the talk soon turned quite naturally to some of the deepest problems of life. Presently a stalwart young Gordon Highlander told of his home in far away Scotland, of his farewell to his dear old mother before he went out to India, and of the promise he made her— the promise he had not kept—to read his Bible every day, to lead a pure clean life, and to keep clear of drink. The atmosphere of that crowded Y.M.C.A. tent had brought it all back to him and, unknown to the staff, he had renewed his vows to God and his mother. In making this confession he was overcome by emotion, and throwing his arms round the leader's neck he sobbed out the story of his repentance. There is no more moving sight than the anguish of a strong man, probably no sight that gives

more joy in Heaven than the tears that tell
of the return of the one that had been lost.

*   *   *

A young Canadian officer who had lost
a leg and an arm wrote to me before sailing
to Montreal from Bristol in May 1918, and
this is what he said :—' I would like to tell
you how much we have appreciated the
Y.M.C.A. I came over with the first batch
of Canadians ; we were drafted to Larkhill,
Salisbury Plain. After leaving my home
—a godly home—I fell into the hands of
very ungodly people and sank very, very
deep in. I was lying on the roadside much
the worse for drink. I was down and
couldn't get up ; comrades and every one
seemed to have left me. I saw one of
your cars rush by. When it had passed
about a hundred yards, out jumped a
Y.M.C.A. man. He came back to me and
said, "Come along my friend, I will take
you to your hut." I looked at him and

said, "I 've sunk too low for a man like you to touch me." He helped me up, took me to my hut, and said, "This is my work in the Y.M.C.A., to help the helpless. Come in and have a cup of tea with me to-morrow." Shamefaced, I went the next day. He was there to greet me ; he talked and prayed with me, but I saw no light until one night in the trenches, I thought I heard this man praying, and I heard it again and again, and had no rest till I laid my sins at the foot of the Cross. Although I am going home with a leg and an arm off, I have a clean heart washed in the Blood of the Lamb. I have visited many huts, but that was the only man who spoke to me personally about my sinful condition. Your leaders can do much if they will. God bless the work and the workers. I will enclose this leader's card so that you can let him know his prayers followed me up to the trenches. God bless him!'

Cecil Thompson, the leader referred to, never saw this letter. Long before it was written he had ' gone west,' had passed to his reward, one of the Red Triangle martyrs of Salisbury Plain. But he ' shall in no wise lose his reward,' for it is work like this that pays, and the spirit of Cecil Thompson lives on in the lives of those who have been won, not by his eloquence, but by the personal contact of a man who had yielded himself to become a channel for the Divine blessing.

*   *   *

The greatest romance of the Red Triangle is the romance of its religious work. War always seems to have one of two effects upon the lives of those who participate in it—either it hardens a man and makes him callous, or else it purifies and ennobles him. The Chaplains, the Churches, the Y.M.C.A., the Church Army, the C.E.T.S., the Salvation Army, and countless other organisations and individuals are always at work, trying to counteract the power of the downward pull. It was our youngest General, the late Brig.-Gen. R. B. Bradford, V.C., M.C., who addressed to his men in France, shortly before his death, the following stirring words :—' I am going to ask you to put your implicit trust and confidence in me, to look upon me not only as your Brigadier, but as your friend. By the help of God I will try and lead you to the best of my ability, and remember your interests are my interests. As you all know, a few days from now we are going to attack ; your powers of endurance are going to be tested. They must not fail you. Above all, pray ; more things are wrought by prayer than this world dreams of. It is God alone who can give us the victory, and bring us through this battle safely.'

*　　*　　*

It is said that General Smuts' attention

was drawn to Herbert Schmalz's picture, 'The Silent Witness,' in the Royal Academy. It showed the interior of a French church, and many wearied and wounded French soldiers huddled together on the floor. A soldier with a wounded arm was awakened by the pain, and raising himself on his unwounded arm saw the figure of the Christ, the silent witness of his suffering and agony. Looking long and earnestly at the picture, it is said the famous Boer General quietly remarked, 'Many a man has seen that vision in this war.'

*　　*　　*

When visiting Bailleul in 1917 the following story was told me by a distinguished padre serving with the Y.M.C.A. It concerned a casualty clearing station on the outskirts of the town. A gentleman ranker was brought in terribly wounded. His shoulder had been shattered by shrapnel and gas gangrene had set in

THE RED TRIANGLE IN JERUSALEM

THE HEXHAM ABBEY HUT, SCHEVINGEN, HOLLAND

SALONICA : WINTER ON THE DOIRAN FRONT, SHOWING Y.M.C.A. TENT

A WELCOME Y.M.C.A. IN THE TRENCHES

A constant and welcome visitor was the senior chaplain. One day he called, and said cheerily, ' Well, old fellow, how goes it to-day ? ' ' Thanks, padre,' was the reply, ' the pain is not quite so bad to-day, but, padre,' he added earnestly, stroking his wounded arm, ' I wish you would persuade them to take this away.' ' Don't talk like that,' said the chaplain ; ' you 'll want to use that old arm for many a year to come ! ' . ' No, padre,' he replied with conviction, ' I shall never use it again ; I 'm going west ! ' A moment later he was seized with a frightful paroxysm of pain, and with a torrent of oaths shrieked out, ' Why the b—— h—— can't they take this arm away ! '. He fell back exhausted, but an instant later sat bolt upright and with arms held out looked intently towards the roof of the hut. His face became radiant, and there was no trace of pain. In an ecstatic voice he cried out, ' Jesus !

P

Jesus! Jesus!' and fell back dead.
Thank God that 's possible, and even in
the hour of death, the blasphemer may
receive forgiveness and the knowledge of
salvation, for

'The ways of men are narrow,
But the gates of Heaven are wide.'

*   *   *

A lady worker in the Isle of Wight felt
unaccountably drawn to a young soldier
who had vowed he would never enter the
Y.M.C.A. again, because he objected to
evening prayers...Little by little she won
his confidence, until the night before he
left for France with a draft, he came in to
say good-bye, and told her she was the first
person to speak to him about sacred things,
adding—'I may do some day, but at
present I cannot see things as you do.' He
went to France, followed by her prayers,
and in due course took part in the famous
attack on Cambrai. Nothing was heard

of him for weeks, and his friends were forced to the conclusion that he was numbered amongst the dead. Time passed by, until one morning the lady of the Red Triangle received a letter from him, written from a German prisoner of war camp. It was a commonplace letter and told of the great fight, of his capture and internment, and so forth, but the concluding words were the ones she wanted—' You will be glad to know I can see things as you do now.'

* . * *

We were speaking at the opening of a hut near Portsmouth. At the close of the ceremony a dear little old widow lady, sitting in the front row, told us of her own boy. He was a young officer serving in France, and was called out late one night to help repel a sudden attack by the enemy. Shot down by machine-gun fire, a brother officer stooped to help him, but he cried, 'Lead on, lead forward, I go to my God!'

*   *   *

A day later another Y.M.C.A. lady in one of the hospital huts told us the story of her nephew. He, too, was a young officer, and was called out to assist in repelling a sudden attack by the Huns. Our men had scarcely reached No Man's Land when the enemy turned on their dreadful gas. One of the first to be overcome by its fumes was the sergeant of his platoon. Regardless of the risk he ran, that young officer stuck to his disabled sergeant until help arrived. Not realising that he had himself become affected by the noxious fumes, he tried to stagger to his feet, but fell backwards into a shell-hole, and in falling broke his neck. The sad news was conveyed to his people in the North of England, and the night they received it his father and mother sat alone in the quiet of their home. Presently the mother spoke—' I feel,' said she, ' that the only thing that would console me in my loss would be to know that the man for whom my boy died was a good man.' It was only a week later that the sergeant for whom the young officer died, came to that home, and when he came he was hopelessly intoxicated. The parents quickly ascertained that it was not the case of a man having been overcome by sudden temptation ; they could have forgiven that, but he was an utter waster, about as bad as a man could be. When he had left the house those two sat once again in the silence of their home, and it was the mother who spoke, slowly and quietly, ' It almost breaks my heart to know my boy gave his precious life for a worthless life like that.' And yet, what of the young officer himself ? Did he know the type of man it was for whom he was about to make the supreme sacrifice? Of course, he knew; he was in his own platoon, and yet, knowing, he willingly gave his life in an attempt to save him. One cannot recall this story without thinking of those wonderful words: 'For scarcely for a righteous man will one die: yet peradventure for a good man some would even dare to die, but God commendeth His Love towards us, in that, while we were yet sinners, Christ died for us.'

* * *

In a far away corner of the Harfleur Valley the Y.M.C.A. has one of its finest equipments. The leader was a great man in every sense of the word, and every night he organised a sing-song for the troops, which invariably went with a swing. He seemed to know by instinct when to strike right in, and what to say. A night came, however, when he seemed to have struck a bad patch, for no one would play, sing, or recite. The story is told here almost word for word, as it was first told me by a leading worker home from France, who drew a graphic word picture of the hut leader pleading from the platform for help which never came. The huge hut was crammed with men, and looking at the crowd standing at the back he noticed a movement amongst them. A trooper detaching himself from the crowd slowly elbowed his way to the front. It was easy to tell by his unsteady steps that he was under the influence of drink. Mounting the platform, he turned first to the audience and then to the Y.M.C.A. leader, and cried in a voice that every one could hear : 'What 's the matter, Boss ? Won't any one oblige you ? Never mind, padre, if nobody will help you, I will ! What would you like me to do ? I can play, or I can sing, or I can recite—or I can pray ! ' For a moment the secretary did not know what to reply. He was a man of experience, but had never been placed in a predicament like that before. To his horror he saw the poor drunken trooper stumble to the edge of the platform and with hands outstretched called for prayer, and there followed one of the strangest prayers ever heard in public as the drunkard cried out, ' Everlasting God! Everlasting God! Everlasting God——! ' He could get no further, but broke down and sobbed like a child, and in his agony cried out, ' I 'd had a good mother once ; I 've been a damned fool. May God forgive me! ' Could God possibly hear and answer a prayer like that? Of course He could, and He did! Possibly He would rather have even a prayer like that, than the meaningless prayers with which we sometimes mock Him, and if any man ever gave evidence of his conversion to God it was that trooper. He stayed only four

Y.M.C.A. FOR INTERNED PRISONERS OF WAR, LEYSIN, SWITZERLAND

days longer in that reinforcement camp in the Harfleur Valley, but if he could help it, never for a moment would he let our leader out of his sight, and in a hundred ways he helped him with his work. He would go methodically and frequently round the hut, gather up the dirty mugs, bring them back to the counter and help to wash them. He would go down on his hands and knees under the tables, pick up scraps of paper and cigarette ends and help clean up the floor. Four days later he was sent with a detachment up the line ; three days later still, with his company, he was ordered ' over the top,' and literally he went into the ' Valley of the Shadow of Death,' but he did not go alone, for ' there went with him One the form of Whom was like unto the form of the Son of God ! '

The Y.M.C.A. is a Christian Association, the Red Triangle a Christian emblem, and for that very reason the freedom of the Association is given to every enlisted man. Protestant and Catholic, Anglican, Free-Churchman, Jew, Hindoo, Mohammedan—men of any religion, every religion, and no religion at all, are equally welcomed beneath its roof, and no man will ever hear unkind or disrespectful things said from a Y.M.C.A. platform concerning the faith he holds dear. At the same time we can never forget that the greatest need of every man, amongst the millions we serve in our huts, is that he should have a Friend who will never fail him nor forsake him, who will stand shoulder to shoulder with him in his fierce fight with temptation in camp or city, will be with him in the trenches, in the firing line, as he goes over the parapet, or even into the dread ' Valley of the Shadow,' and there is only One Who can thus meet every need of every man, and that One is the strong Son of God, the Lord

Jesus Christ, the best Friend, the truest Comrade we can have.

We often fall far short of our aim, alas! but the primary aim of the Y.M.C.A. always has been, and is, to lead men to a saving knowledge of that Friend.

CHAPTER XVIII

THE RED TRIANGLE IN THE RECONSTRUCTION

The Y.M.C.A. has a very thorough understanding of men, and with that sympathy which has characterised its work throughout has brought to the National Employment Exchange system an element which has humanised the movement.

The state of the Labour Market and the condition of trade after the lapse of the period of reconstruction following the war will be so favourable that the physically fit man will experience little difficulty in securing employment, but even if that is so we shall, for a long time, have with us the disabled man, who, without assistance and guidance, cannot be suitably placed in industry. We must see an extension of the good-will and sympathy evinced by the Y.M.C.A. movement amongst every class in the community.

The Advisory Committee of the Ministry of Labour are getting up a special department to deal with the discharged soldier. What the Y.M.C.A. contributes to this problem is character.—MR. G. H. ROBERTS, M.P., MINISTER OF LABOUR.

THE question is often asked ' What is going to be done with the Y.M.C.A. huts after the war ? ' It is never easy to prophesy with any degree of certainty, but there can be little doubt that, properly handled, these huts will be at least as useful after the war as they are now. Their furniture, which comprises hundreds of billiard tables, thousands of chairs, tables, stoves, ranges, and so forth, is well fitted for doing good service after the war. One of these huts planted down in the centre of some rural community and staffed by voluntary workers, who have purchased their experience by downright hard service during the war, should be an inestimable boon. It would break the monotony of country life ; or, being set down in an industrial district of a big town or city, would help in congenial ways to relieve the tedium of the drab life of the workers.

The immediate problem is that of the discharged man. Incidentally his presence in our midst is even now helping us to gain that practical acquaintance with his needs that will be invaluable in dealing with the greater problem of demobilisation. Thousands of men are discharged from the Navy and Army every week. Many of these for months, it may be for years to come, will not be able to do a good day's work, no matter how willing they may be, and it is up to us to help them. No one who has seen the conditions under which they have been living in Picardy or in Flanders can wonder at this, and they will need sympathy and encouragement on the part of their employers. The Y.M.C.A. can supply the human touch that may be of the greatest possible service to the Ministries of Labour, Pensions, and Reconstruction, and although the State itself must take responsibility for the future of those who return broken from the war and for their dependents, there will still be ample room for voluntary effort without any taint of charity.

A number of experiments are being tried, all designed to point the way to future efforts if such experiments prove successful. The Red Triangle Farm Colony at Kinson in Dorset has been fitted up as a sanatorium for the benefit of men discharged from the Navy and Army who need sanatorium treatment because they are suffering from, or threatened with, consumption, and whilst the men are undergoing treatment they are trained in poultry-farming, horticulture, and other outdoor pursuits on plans cordially approved by the authorities.

A Red Triangle Poultry Farm in Surrey is also run entirely for the benefit of discharged men, and a somewhat larger venture is under way in Suffolk with a two hundred acre farm and extensive fruit gardens. At Portsmouth and other centres hostel accommodation is provided for men who, on leaving the Navy or Army, go through a course of training for civil life.

Experimental workshops in London are proving a great success, discharged soldiers being trained in carpentry, joinery, picture-framing, and the repairing of pianos.

A series of exhibitions dealing with the work of ex-soldiers has been successfully inaugurated, and Red Triangle employment bureaux have already secured situations for more than twenty thousand discharged men.

The biggest opportunity for the Red Triangle will come with the declaration of peace. ' After the war ' for tens of thousands of men has commenced already, and not only during the war, but in the reconstruction we shall need the help of every worker who is prepared heart and soul to work out the full programme of the Red Triangle for Britain's sake and for the sake of the Kingdom of God.

Printed in Great Britain by T. and A. CONSTABLE, Printers to His Majesty
at the Edinburgh University Press